Simple C

Simple C

Jim McGregor
Richard McGregor
Alan Watt

ADDISON-WESLEY

HARLOW, ENGLAND ■ READING, MASSACHUSETTS

MENLO PARK, CALIFORNIA ■ NEW YORK ■ DON MILLS, ONTARIO

AMSTERDAM ■ BONN ■ SYDNEY ■ SINGAPORE ■ TOKYO ■ MADRID

SAN JUAN ■ MILAN ■ MEXICO CITY ■ SEOUL ■ TAIPEI

© Addison Wesley Longman 1998
Addison Wesley Longman Limited
Edinburgh Gate
Harlow
Essex CM20 2JE
England

and Associated Companies throughout the World.

The rights of Jim McGregor, Richard McGregor and Alan Watt to be identified as
authors of this Work have been asserted by them in accordance with the Copyright,
Designs and Patents Act 1988.

The programs in this book have been included for their instructional value. They have
been tested with care but are not guaranteed for any particular purpose. The publisher
does not offer any warranties or representations nor does it accept any liabilities with
respect to the programs.

Many of the designations used by manufacturers and sellers to distinguish their products
are claimed as trademarks. Addison Wesley Longman Limited has made every attempt to
supply trademark information about manufacturers and their products mentioned in this
book.

Cover designed by ODB Design & Communication, Reading
and printed by The Riverside Printing Co (Reading) Ltd.
Text design by Claire Brodmann
Typeset in 9.5/12pt Stone Serif by 30
Printed and bound in Great Britain by Biddles Ltd., Guildford and King's Lynn

First printed 1997

ISBN 0-201-40385-4

British Library Cataloguing-in-Publication Data
A catalogue record for this book is available from the British Library

Trademark Notice
The following are trademarks or registered trademarks of their respective companies:
Java is a trademark of Sun Microsystems Inc.

Library of Congress Cataloging-in-Publication Data
McGregor, James J. , 1946–
    Simple C / Jim McGregor, Richard McGregor, Alan Watt.
       p.   cm.
    Includes index.
    ISBN 0–201–40385–4 (alk. paper)
    1. C (Computer program language)   I. McGregor, Richard.
II. Watt, Alan H. , 1942–   III. Title.
QA76.73.C15M369 1997
005. 13'3 – – dc21
                                        97–21933
                                           CIP

Contents

Preface

Although many computer users find preprogrammed packages such as word processors and spreadsheets sufficient for their computing needs, many others have a need to exercise greater control over the computer's behaviour by writing their own computer programs.

About the book

The purpose of this book is to provide an introduction on how to write computer programs in C, one of the most widely-used programming languages. It is intended to be a genuine introductory text for beginners. The main problem encountered by beginners is in expressing what they want the computer to do, in terms of the available instructions in the programming language being used. For this reason we aim to teach C programming without presenting more information about the internal workings of the computer than is absolutely necessary. Unnecessary use of computing jargon is also avoided.

We do not attempt to cover the complete C language, but concentrate on a central part that is adequate for writing a wide range of useful programs. The material covered will be sufficient for the needs of the casual programmer who needs to occasionally use the computer for problem solving. A mastery of the material in this book will also provide a solid foundation on which to base further study of advanced programming techniques and of Computer Science in general.

Throughout the book the fundamental ideas are introduced by means of examples. At first the examples are simple programs that may not seem convincingly useful. We must ask the reader to be patient: a clear understanding of the elementary techniques introduced in these examples is essential before programs of real practical use can be written. We believe that programming is a skill learned mainly by reading and writing programs and we urge the reader to attempt most of the exercises set at the end of each chapter.

How the book is organised

In the Introduction we present some of the basic concepts involved in programming. We use a very simple C program to introduce the ideas involved.

Chapters 1 and 2 describe the programming constructions that are used to program the computer to read data, do straightforward calculations and display the results.

Chapters 3, 4 and 5 present the C constructions that enable us to control the order in which the computer carries out its calculations, for example, by choosing between several courses of action on the basis of tests, or by repeating blocks of instructions many times. It is this ability to control the order in which a program is obeyed that gives the computer much of its power.

Chapters 6 and 7 examine techniques for organising the various constructions introduced so far into more complex programs.

Finally, in Chapters 8, 9 and 10 we focus on organising the data that can be manipulated by a program. The same techniques that were demonstrated previously with numeric data are applied to text and other collections of data values.

Conventions used in the book

- New terminology is introduced in **bold type**.
- Complete programs are displayed in `Courier fixed width font`.
- Fragments of C code in the text also appear in `Courier fixed width font`.
- Interaction between a program and the user is also displayed in `Courier fixed width font` and material typed by the user is displayed in **bold type**.
- Outline descriptions of subproblems, yet to be coded in detail, appear in *italics*.

Web access to the example programs

The example programs can be downloaded from the following web address:

http://www.dcs.shef.ac.uk/~jjm/simplec

Comments on the book

Any comments on the material in the book can be sent by email to the authors at:

J.McGregor@dcs.shef.ac.uk

Jim McGregor
Richard McGregor
Alan Watt
Sheffield, May 1997

Introduction

A computer program is a set of instructions that tells a computer how to carry out a calculation or perform some other operation. You will often find computer programs referred to as the **software** of the computer, to distinguish them from the **hardware** (the chips, circuit boards, wiring and so on). In this chapter, we shall discuss some of the background to the programming task and introduce your first C program.

▉ Why program at all?

The first question a beginner might ask is: why learn to program at all? Why not simply use one of the many pieces of commercial software available – a word processor, a spreadsheet or a database system – to store and process text and data? The answer is that, for many computer users, this would be a perfectly adequate solution. However, the computer packages mentioned above do not always provide all of the features that are needed by a computer user. Everyone who is more than a casual computer user, scientists and non-scientists alike, will frequently be faced with a problem to solve that requires a tailor-made program. People find that an ability to write programs can save hours of manual calculation or data processing, or fruitless and time-consuming attempts to persuade a spreadsheet or database package to carry out tasks that it was not designed to do.

Another reason for learning to write programs might simply be to acquire a very marketable skill. Computer packages such as those mentioned above, as well as the computer games that flood the market, are constantly being written and rewritten by the vast and growing army of professional programmers, whose skills put them in high demand.

A third reason, and one that drives many programmers, is that programming is in itself an intellectual challenge. Immense satisfaction is obtained from conceiving and implementing a complex computer program, whatever the application area.

■ Why C?

The instructions that constitute a computer program have to be expressed in one of the many computer programming languages available. C is one such language, and is probably one of the most widely used at the present time. An enormous proportion of computer software currently in use is written in C. Another widely used programming language is C++, an object-oriented programming (OOP) language that has been developed from C. A discussion of OOP is beyond the scope of this book, but any future attempt to learn C++ will require a thorough understanding of the fundamental concepts present in C, thus providing another motivation for the ambitious beginner to learn C.

A programming language that has suddenly become fashionable, for very good reasons, is Java. This is a language specifically designed for writing programs that can be run easily on any type of computer, regardless of the hardware system originally used to develop the program – a tremendous advantage when developing software that is to be transmitted across the World Wide Web. Java is another object-oriented language that contains most of the features of C. However, the designers of Java have omitted the features of C that make it prone to errors when used by careless programmers.

To conclude, C is a programming language that is still widely used in its own right. For the programmer who will eventually move on to programming in C++ or Java, a thorough grounding in the main features of C will still be essential.

■ The programming environment

If you are going to learn to program in C, you need to have available one of the many C programming environments. A C program, as written by the programmer, is simply a piece of text containing the programmer's instructions for the computer. Of course, these instructions will have been written according to the very precise rules for the C language – the main topic for the rest of this book.

The first step in communicating your program to the computer is to type it at the keyboard, in just the same way that you would type a piece of text into a word processor. In fact, some programmers use their favourite word processor for initially typing the text of a new program. It is more likely that you will be using some kind of **integrated development environment** specially designed for programming in C. This will include an editor that enables you to type and edit the text of your programs and store them in files. Additional commands will enable you to tell the computer to obey your program once it has been typed. Obeying the program is often referred to as **running** or **executing** the program. Until relatively recently, editing packages and software for running programs were separate.

Running a C program involves first translating or **compiling** it into a form of executable code that the hardare of your particular computer can deal with – the **machine code** for your computer. This will be done automatically for you in an integrated environment, as soon as you ask for your program to be run. A further stage of **linking** will also take place in order to link your program to any of the standard program libraries that may have been used. Details of these processes need not concern you at this stage – it will suffice for you to be familiar with the terminology in order to interpret certain error messages that may be produced by your C system. If you are not using an integrated environment, you may need to type separate commands to compile, link and then run your program.

At this stage, it will assist further discussion if we present a simple example of a C program.

■ A simple C program

The following very simple C program will be used to illustrate a number of fundamental points. We shall explain shortly what this program tells the computer to do.

```
#include <stdio.h>

void main (void)
{
   printf("Your room needs %i square metres of carpet\n", 3*2 );
   printf("and %i square metres of wallpaper.\n", 2*(3+2)*3 );
}
```

We must first type this program into the computer from the keyboard. Note that the case (capital or small letters) of the text you type is important in C. For instance, in the program above, `printf` must occur in lower-case text in order to be recognized.

Once the program has been typed into the computer, the computer can be asked to obey it.

The first line of our introductory program:

```
#include <stdio.h>
```

will be explained in more detail later, but for the moment we can understand it as telling the computer that the program which follows will use some of the functions from the standard input–output library (to write to the screen, for example).

The part of the program that tells the computer what to do is enclosed between the two lines:

```
{
```

and

```
}
```

Any part of a program enclosed between two curly brackets or **braces** like these is known as a **block**, and your C programs should always contain a block preceded by the heading:

```
void main (void)
```

This constitutes a **function** called 'main'. Every C program must have a `main` function – it is used as the starting point whenever the computer obeys the program.

So `main` contains a list of **statements** (only two in this case), each of which is terminated with a semicolon. The first statement obeyed in this program is:

```
printf("Your room needs %i square metres of carpet\n", 3*2 );
```

This tells the computer to 'print' or display the information specified between the round brackets, or **parentheses**, as they are called in C. The information output will usually be displayed on the computer screen. The text between the quotation marks is a **formatting string**. This will be displayed exactly as it stands, except for the two pairs of characters `%i` and `\n`. These are **formatting codes** which have the following meaning:

- `%i`: when the text is displayed, `%i` will be replaced with the value of the **expression** that occurs after the text – in this case, `3*2`, which evaluates to 6 (we use `*` as a multiplication sign). `%i` means that the information will be displayed as an **integer** or whole number. We shall encounter other examples used for displaying different types of information later.
- `\n`: this pair of characters indicates that any subsequent output is to be produced at the start of a new line.

When the computer has obeyed one statement, it goes on to the next:

```
printf("and %i square metres of wallpaper.\n", 2*(3+2)*3 );
```

Again, the `%i` marks the point in the text at which the value of the expression `2*(3+2)*3` will be inserted. The parentheses in this expression have the usual arithmetic interpretation. Thus, when the computer obeys our introductory program, it will display the floor area and wall area of a 3 m × 2 m × 3 m room:

```
Your room needs 6 square metres of carpet
and 30 square metres of wallpaper.
```

Perhaps we should mention at this point that many C programmers use `%d` instead of `%i`, and you will often see this. In the original definition of C, `%d` (for decimal) was used for printing an integer. The modern ANSI standard C specifies that `%i` is the code for printing an integer, and this is what we shall use.

In order for the computer to be able to process a program, a language like C must have strict rules about the sequence of symbols that make up statements and programs. This is called the **syntax** of the language. The rules for program layout are less strict. We can insert as many spaces as we like between the words, symbols and numbers in the program, providing that words are separated by at least one space. We are also free to choose how we set the program out on separate lines, as long as we do not start a new line in the middle of a word or number. We shall make use of this freedom of layout to make our programs as readable as possible. This is very important, not only because we may wish someone else to read and understand our programs, but also because we may wish to re-read them ourselves at some later date when we want to extend or modify them.

In discussing the behaviour of the introductory program, we have assumed that it has been typed correctly. What happens if a mistake is made when writing or typing the program?

▇ Types of error

The first type of error that can occur will prevent your program from running at all. For instance, if you put a comma or semicolon in the wrong place, the computer might report that there is a **syntax error** in your program and will not be able to obey it. Most errors like this would be detected by the compiler, but some may be reported as linking errors. For example, if you misspelt the word `printf`, the linker would be unable to find the required output function.

There are many errors that can be made in a C program that go undetected by the computer because the program is grammatically or **syntactically** correct. Such an error could be the result of a simple typing mistake, or it could be the result of a faulty logical analysis of the original problem. When the program is obeyed, its behaviour will not be what you intended. One outcome of this could be that the program will fail and terminate while it is being obeyed. For example, the result of a calculation may be a number that is too big for the computer to handle. If such a **run-time error** occurs, the computer will stop obeying your program and display a message explaining what has happened.

Finally, a program that contains errors may still run successfully and, of course, this does not necessarily mean that correct answers have been produced. If, in our introductory program, we mistyped the expression for the wall area as `2*(3-2)*3`, telling the computer to subtract the length of our room from its width, the computer would still successfully obey the program. It would display:

```
Your room needs 6 square metres of carpet
and 6 square metres of wallpaper.
```

which is of course wrong. This is why **testing** is such an important stage in program development.

▇ Program data

Programs, once written, can be obeyed over and over again, and this is one of the main advantages of a computer. We could, for instance, write a weekly payroll program that is run 52 times a year. Our introductory example is not very useful, however, because if it were obeyed again it would produce exactly the same output.

Programs are usually written in more general terms so that the calculations described in them can be performed on different numbers, or **data**, on different occasions. For example, a payroll program would have to be given the number of hours worked by each employee during the current week, current rates of pay, and so on.

Our 'Room' program calculates the floor and wall areas for a room with particular dimensions. A program that could perform the same calculations, but for different rooms on different occasions, would be more generally useful. Making a program general in this sense is one of the main topics of Chapter 1.

■ Testing and debugging

The importance of testing a computer program was mentioned above. In our introductory program, there was very little testing we could do apart from running the program and checking the answer. When a program is written so that it can be given different data each time it is used, the need for testing the program becomes more vital. Before we can be confident that a program is producing the correct answers to realistic problems, we must test it thoroughly on a range of data that represents problems for which we know the answer.

The process of removing errors from a program is often referred to as **debugging**. The bugs in a program can be caused by many different types of errors, and you will gradually gather experience in recognizing likely causes. At the end of each chapter in the rest of the book, we have given some advice about common programming problems and how to track down the causes.

■ Programming in the large

The main thrust of this book is unashamedly to teach you to write code in C, and we will concentrate on giving you a thorough grounding in the programming process at this level. However, before we continue, we must look briefly at the wider issues involved in the implementation of large software projects. Such a project might require hundreds or thousands of person-years of effort and can easily match, in scale and complexity, engineering problems such as designing and building a large bridge, the Channel Tunnel or a new aircraft. The consequences of software failure can be just as disastrous as the failure of a large engineering artefact – software is used to control everything from washing machines and automobiles through to chemical plants, nuclear power stations and space missions. Failure of financial and management software could spell commercial disaster for a company and could result in unemployment for thousands of employees, or even a stockmarket crash followed by global recession! The subjects of computer science and software engineering are concerned with the development and use of **methodologies** for specifying, designing and implementing large pieces of software, as well as techniques for managing such large software projects. What you will learn in this book will be only a beginning if you should move on to work on large programming projects like these.

Even at the level of the material covered in this book, you will need to adopt a fairly disciplined approach to writing programs, particularly from Chapter 6 onwards. In Chapter 6, we therefore demonstrate an approach to designing programs that will help at this level. If you then move on to larger programming tasks, you will we hope – take with you an understanding of the underlying themes of structure, good practice and problem solving.

CHAPTER 1

Getting information
in and out

In this chapter, we describe various ways of getting information into and out of the computer while a program is being obeyed.

1.1 ■ Getting information into a program

As we saw in the Introduction, the line of code:

```
printf("Your room needs %i square metres of carpet\n", 3*2 );
```

causes the computer to write or display:

```
Your room needs 6 square metres of carpet
```

When the statement is obeyed, the formatting string between the quotation marks is written with the value 6 substituted where the %i occurs.

In order to make our introductory program more flexible, consider:

```
printf("Your room needs %i square metres of carpet\n", length*width);
```

in which we have replaced a particular expression, 3*2, by a more general one: length*width. In the program, length and width are going to be the names of two **variables**. We can think of a variable as a named box in which a program can store something:

length $\boxed{3}$ width $\boxed{2}$

We can say that length is the name of a box containing 3 and width is the name of a box containing 2. We shall soon see how these values get there. When the computer evaluates the expression length*width, it multiplies the *contents* of length by the *contents* of width. Of course, the boxes length and width need not necessarily contain the numbers 3 and 2. They could contain any numbers that are not too big for the size of the box (more about that later); for example:

length 50   width 35

This is why we use the term 'variable'. Now we can rewrite our introductory program in such a way that, each time it is run or obeyed, different numbers may be put in the boxes length and width. This gives us Program 1.1.

PROGRAM 1.1

This program works out the amount of floor and wall covering required for a room of *any* length, width and height.

```
/* Program 1.1 : Room Size */

#include <stdio.h>

void main (void)
{
   int length, width, height;

   scanf("%i%i%i", &length, &width, &height);
   printf("Your room needs %i square metres of carpet\n",
                                        length*width);
   printf("and %i square metres of wallpaper.\n",
                              2*(length+width)*height);

}
```

The very first line of Program 1.1 contains the name of the program and is called a **comment**. We can also insert comments that explain to the human reader what the program is supposed to be doing. Any group of characters enclosed between /* and */ are displayed as part of the program but have no effect on its behaviour when it is obeyed. Comments should be inserted in a program wherever they make it easier to understand. This would be important if someone else is likely to have to take over your program and modify it, or if you yourself are likely to have to modify it at some future date when the details of how it works have been forgotten. Comments are kept to a minimum throughout this book since each example program is discussed extensively in the text.

Observe that each printf statement has been spread over two lines. A statement can be broken up with spaces or new lines without changing its meaning, as long as we do not break the statement in the middle of a word, a number or a string.

The first line within function main in Program 1.1 simply tells the computer to set aside space for three variables, length, width and height. int is short for 'integer' and this means that these variables can hold only integers or whole numbers – in this example we assume that our room dimensions will be given as a whole number of metres. More information about this appears in Section 1.3.

The statement:

```
scanf("%i%i%i", &length, &width, &height);
```

is the means whereby particular values are put in the boxes `length`, `width` and `height` each time the program is run. Be sure to include the `&` symbol that precedes each of the three names. We must tell the `scanf` function *where to put* the values that will be supplied and the `&` symbol is used to do this. When the computer obeys this statement it pauses and waits until three numbers are supplied. We shall assume, for the time being, that such numbers are supplied directly from a keyboard while the computer is obeying the program (Figure 1.1).

The program then continues execution and evaluates the general expressions:

```
length*width
```

and

```
2*(length+width)*height
```

using the values for `length`, `width` and `height` that are now contained in the boxes with these names. These are the values that have just been supplied from the keyboard. The values supplied as input are sometimes called the **data** for the program. When numbers are typed as input for a program, they are separated by spaces (as many as we like) or spread over as many lines as we like by using the Enter key. The data for each `scanf` statement must be terminated by the Enter key. Punctuation such as commas or other non-numeric characters should not be included in numeric input. Your program will probably run, but the values inserted in the variables will be unpredictable and the results produced by the program will be wrong. You should also avoid putting characters other than the `%` codes in the formatting string for `scanf`.

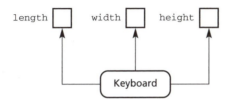

Figure 1.1 Values needed by the program are supplied from the keyboard.

1.2 ■ Using a program

After you have typed a program it is stored in a way peculiar to your own system. Perhaps you have used an editor that is part of an integrated C package. If that is the case, there will be an option under one of the menus to compile and run (or execute) your program. The result of running Program 1.1 should be a display like:

```
3    2    3
Your room needs 6 square metres of carpet
and 30 square metres of wallpaper.
```

The line in bold was typed by the person using the program (the 'user') and the remainder by the computer. Of course, Program 1.1 could be re-run using different values. This might produce the following:

```
5    3    3
Your room needs 15 square metres of carpet
and 48 square metres of wallpaper.
```

When a program is to be controlled from a keyboard as above, it is good programming practice to precede a scanf statement with a printf statement that displays a message telling or reminding the user what to type next. If we run a particular program months after it has been written, or if another person (not the programmer) runs the program, then it is vital that the program informs the user what information is to be typed and in what order.

━━━━━━━━━━━━━━━ **PROGRAM 1.2** ━━━━━━━━━━━━━━━

This is identical to Program 1.1 except that the program will type a request for input when it is required.

```c
/* Program 1.2 : Room Size 2 */

#include <stdio.h>

void main (void)
{
   int length, width, height;

   printf("Type in length, width and height:\n");
   scanf("%i%i%i", &length, &width, &height);
   printf("Your room needs %i square metres of carpet\n",
                                     length*width);
   printf("and %i square metres of wallpaper.\n",
                              2*(length+width)*height);
}
```

This has been done in Program 1.2, which will produce a display like the following:

```
Type in length, width and height:
3  2  4
Your room needs 6 square metres of carpet
and 40 square metres of wallpaper.
```

The appearance of the first line in the display serves as a **prompt** to remind a user of the program what information is required.

An interesting and useful variation would be to use three prompts and three scanf statements:

```
printf("Type in length:"); scanf("%i", &length);
printf("Type in width:");  scanf("%i", &width);
printf("Type in height:"); scanf("%i", &height);
```

with the user pressing the Enter key after each value supplied as input.

1.3 ■ Variables and declarations

In Programs 1.1 and 1.2 the line:

```
int length, width, height;
```

gives the computer three pieces of information:

■ You require three boxes or variables.

■ The names of these boxes are to be length, width and height.

■ You are going to put quantities in these boxes that are integer numbers, or whole numbers.

This is called a **variable declaration**; in its simplest form it comprises two parts:

(1) The type of quantity the box is going to contain. For the moment we are going to use only two types, int and float. A float (short for floating point) value is a number with a fractional part. Floating point numbers and integers are represented in different ways inside the computer, and there are good reasons for distinguishing between them in a program. int variables are generally used in a program for counting things and float variables are used for holding the results of arithmetic calculations.

(2) A list of names chosen by the programmer, separated by commas. A name consists of a sequence of letters and numeric digits, starting with a letter. Underline characters can also be included. C keywords like int must not be used as variable names. A complete list of keywords is given in Appendix A. At this stage, you do not need to know what all the keywords mean but you must not attempt to use them as variable names.

You should choose meaningful names. For example, in the above context we used the names `length`, `width` and `height` rather than `l`, `w` and `h`, or, worse still, `x`, `y` and `z`. This makes it much easier for your program to be read by other people or by yourself in the future if you wish to develop it further. Names can be of any length but you may find your particular computer system specifies a maximum length. Spaces must not be typed in the middle of a word, but this is not too inconvenient; it means you must use, for example, `numberoftimes`, `NumberOfTimes` or `number_of_times` rather than `number of times`. The precise way in which you type long variable names is largely a matter of personal taste. In this book, we shall use a mixture of conventions – if the meaning is fairly clear, we shall simply use lower-case letters, but we will occasionally use upper-case letters or underline characters. If you use a name that includes upper-case letters, do not forget that the name must be typed in the same way whenever it appears in your program – C is **case sensitive**.

Now consider the following examples:

```
int years, months;
```

means that the program is going to use two variables called `years` and `months`, which are going to contain integers; for example:

years $\boxed{53}$ months $\boxed{4}$

The following declaration:

```
float temperature;
```

means that the program is going to use a variable called `temperature`, which is going to contain a floating point number; for example:

temperature $\boxed{93.75}$

The following declarations:

```
int years, months;
float temperature;
```

mean that the program is going to use three variables, two of which are going to contain integers and one a floating point number.

There is a limit to the maximum size of integer that can be put in an `int` variable, and similarly a limit to the maximum size of floating point number that can be put in a `float` variable. These limits can vary from system to system, but `int` should allow whole numbers up to at least 32 767. A `float` variable should be able to store very large and very small numbers with at least six digits of precision. These restrictions can be overcome by using the type `long int` for larger integers and `double` for **double precision** floating point numbers. A `long int` can be read and printed with the `%li` formatting code (note that it is the *letter* l between % and `i`). Both `float` and `double` values are read and printed with `%f`.

Program 1.3 illustrates the use of `float` variables. In this program the formatting strings in the `scanf` and `printf` statements use `%f`, which must always be used when we want to read or write a floating point number.

PROGRAM 1.3

The outstanding debt on a loan is increased each month by a percentage (the monthly rate of interest), and decreased by that month's payment. This program calculates the outstanding debt on a loan after a monthly payment has been made.

```
/* Program 1.3 : Loan Repayment */

#include <stdio.h>

void main (void)
{
   float debt, MonthlyRate, payment;

   printf("debt?"); scanf("%f", &debt);
   printf("monthly rate?"); scanf("%f", &MonthlyRate);
   printf("repayment?"); scanf("%f", &payment);
   printf("Debt after next payment is ");
   printf("%f\n", debt + debt*MonthlyRate/100 - payment);

}
```

You should note that this is a very simple program, which does not take into account the fact that the payment may be greater than the outstanding debt. This possibility will be dealt with in subsequent chapters.

1.4 ■ Getting information out of a program: Simple output

Up to now we have been using printf in various contexts where it seems reasonably obvious from the context what the effect will be. We shall now look in more detail at the behaviour of such printf statements.

Consider the following examples:

Statement	Computer displays
`printf("Hello!\n")`	Hello!
`printf("%i\n", 25)`	25
`printf("%i\n", 3*2)`	6
`printf("3 x 2 = %i\n", 3*2)`	3 x 2 = 6

From these examples we can see that:

■ A printf statement always includes at least one thing to be displayed, a formatting string enclosed in quotation marks.

■ There may be other items after the string, separated by commas. The string should contain information about how to display the values of any such items.
■ The computer may perform a calculation to obtain a value to be displayed.

Here are two more examples. We assume that length contains 5 and width contains 3.

Statement	Computer displays
`printf("%i\n", length*width);`	15
`printf("Area is %i\n", length*width);`	Area is 15

Of course, an entity after the formatting string can be just a single variable name. For example, if the variables i and j contain the numbers shown:

i ⬚7⬚   j ⬚2⬚

Statement	Computer displays
`printf("%i\n", i);`	7
`printf("%i\n", j);`	2
`printf("i contains %i\n", i);`	i contains 7
`printf("j contains %i\n", j);`	j contains 2

You should also examine carefully the differences in the effects of the following four statements:

```
printf("sum of i & j is %i\n", i+j);        sum of i & j is 9
printf("sum of %i & %i is %i\n", i, j, i+j);  sum of 7 & 2 is 9
printf("i + j = %i\n", i+j);                i + j = 9
printf("%i + %i = %i\n", i, j, i+j);        7 + 2 = 9
```

In the absence of formatting information (as discussed in the next section) any values in a printf statement will be displayed in a standard way. We shall assume throughout this book that, when %i and %f are used in this way, int numbers and float numbers are displayed without any additional spaces before or after, and that float numbers are displayed with six digits after the decimal point. Thus, we shall assume that:

```
printf("%i and %f\n", 2*3, 65.734*2);
```

produces

```
6 and 131.468000
```

We have seen \n occur frequently in printf statements. As we said in the Introduction, this causes further output to come at the start of a new line. It is possible to have more than one occurrence of \n in a piece of text to be displayed. For example:

```
printf("1st line\n2nd line\n3rd line\n");
```

will display

```
1st line
2nd line
3rd line
```

To start a new line without displaying any other characters, we can use:

```
printf("\n");
```

on its own. This does not necessarily imply that a blank line is displayed. For example:

Statements	Computer displays

`printf("1st line");`
`printf("\n");`
`printf("2nd line\n");`
	`1st line`
	`2nd line`

`printf("1st line\n");`
`printf("\n");`
`printf("3rd line\n");`
	`1st line`
	
	`3rd line`

═══════════════ **PROGRAM 1.4** ═══════════════

This program draws a simple triangle of stars on the screen.

```
/* Program 1.4 : Triangle */

#include <stdio.h>

void main (void)
{
  printf("                    *\n");
  printf("                  *   *\n");
  printf("                *       *\n");
  printf("              *           *\n");
  printf("            *               *\n");
  printf("          *     triangle      *\n");
  printf("        *                       *\n");
  printf("      *                           *\n");
  printf("* * * * * * * * * * * * * * * *\n");
}
```

Program 1.4 uses `printf` statements to draw a simple pattern of characters on the screen. Note that this is a program to which we do not supply any input information. Neither does the program use any variables.

Program 1.5 is a first attempt to display an electricity bill that looks, for example, like this:

```
*****************************
Present meter reading     6015
Previous meter reading    5899
Units used                 116
Rate per unit             6.73 pence
Standing charge          £7.78

The sum due is           £15.59
*****************************
```

We have made use of extra spaces in the strings in an attempt to line up the column of numbers displayed by the computer on the right. You will find it difficult in this type of context to get the precise layout you want without the use of the facilities discussed in the next section.

Unfortunately, the figure displayed on the last line (the total sum due) will not be in the format we require; there will be four extra digits displayed after the price, since six digits are displayed to the right of the decimal point when we use the %f format. This is another reason why we need the formatting facilities of the next section.

PROGRAM 1.5

This program displays an electricity bill, given a present meter reading and a previous meter reading. The price per unit (in pence) and a fixed standing charge are constant. The units used and the sum due are to be calculated.

```c
/* Program 1.5 : Electricity Bill */
#include <stdio.h>
void main (void)
{
  int present, previous;
  printf("Type present and previous meter readings:\n");
  scanf("%i%i", &present, &previous);
  printf("*****************************\n");
  printf("Present meter reading    %i\n", present);
  printf("Previous meter reading   %i\n", previous);
  printf("Units used                  %i\n", present-previous);
  printf("Rate per unit            6.73 pence\n");
  printf("Standing charge          £7.78\n\n");
  printf("The sum due is           £");
  printf("%f\n", (present-previous)*6.73/100 + 7.78);
  printf("*****************************\n");
}
```

We shall see in Chapter 3 how to take into account the fact that the previous meter reading could be greater than the present meter reading if the meter has gone through its maximum of 10000, say, and reset to zero.

We have again used parentheses (round brackets) in Program 1.5, where their meaning should be fairly obvious. The use of parentheses in expressions like these will be explained fully in Chapter 2. Note that the symbol / means 'divided by', not to be confused with the \ of \n.

1.5 ■ Getting information out of a program: Formatted output

We can supply more information about the layout we require for the values output by printf statements. This is done by providing formatting information as part of the %i or %f in the string passed to printf. For example:

```
printf("...%8i...\n", 2*256);
```

when obeyed will display:

```
...     512...
```

with five additional spaces inserted before the number. The value 512 requires only three character widths when displayed, but in this example we have instructed the computer to make the total number of characters up to a **field width** of 8, if necessary, by inserting additional spaces before the value displayed. Each %i in the string can contain formatting information between the % and the i. (If more than the specified number of characters is needed, the number will still be displayed, but of course no extra spaces are inserted.)

The formatting facility is very useful when output values are being lined up in columns. For example, given a variable j that contains 97, the following:

```
printf("   i  i*j\n");
printf("\n");
printf("%4i%6i\n", 1, j);
printf("%4i%6i\n", 25, 25*j);
printf("%4i%6i\n", 125, 125*j);
```

will display:

```
  i   i*j

  1    97
 25  2425
125 12125
```

In the case of floating point values, two format numbers can be provided, separated by a '.' character. The first indicates the field width – the minimum number of characters to be displayed altogether. The second indicates the **precision** – the number of digits to be displayed after the decimal point.

Thus, if a variable x contains 9.479 and y contains 3.141592:

```
printf("%8.4f%9.4f%9.2f%10.3f\n", x, y, x+y, y-x);
```

will display

```
  9.4790   3.1416    12.62    -6.337
[......][.......][.......][........]
```

(The second line is just to help you count the characters.) The number of characters displayed includes the decimal point and the minus sign, if any. The value of y has been **rounded** to give four digits after the decimal point (and not truncated).

Occasionally it is convenient to omit the field width and simply specify the precision for a floating point number. For example, if a value is being output as part of a sentence, we do not usually require extra spaces to be included. Thus, if pi has been given the value 3.141592:

```
printf("The value of pi to 3 decimal places is %.3f\n", pi);
```

will display:

```
The value of pi to 3 decimal places is 3.142
```

1.6 ■ Named constants

Named constants are values to which names are given before a program is obeyed. Such values remains unchanged during the execution of the program and cannot be altered.

In Program 1.6, you can see that named constants are defined at the start of the program and that the definition takes the form:

```
#define NAME value
```

═══════════ **PROGRAM 1.6** ═══════════

This program displays the area and circumference of a circle of given radius.

```
/* Program 1.6 : Area Of Circle */
#include <stdio.h>
#define PI 3.14159

void main (void)
{
  float radius;
  printf("Radius of circle?");
  scanf("%f", &radius);
  printf("The circumference is %5.3f\n", 2*PI*radius);
  printf("The area is          %5.3f\n", PI*radius*radius);
}
```

Program 1.7, a rewrite of Program 1.5, illustrates the use of named constants, as well as the use of formatted output.

PROGRAM 1.7

This program displays an electricity bill, given present and previous meter readings.

```c
/* Program 1.7 : Electricity Bill 2 */

#include <stdio.h>
#define UNITRATE 6.73
#define STANDCHARGE 7.78
#define ASTERISKS "*****************************\n"

void main (void)
{
   int present, previous;

   printf("Type present and previous meter readings:\n");
   scanf("%i%i", &present, &previous);
   printf(ASTERISKS);
   printf("Present meter reading %7i\n", present);
   printf("Previous meter reading%7i\n", previous);
   printf("Units used            %7i\n", present-previous);
   printf("Rate per unit         %7.2f pence\n", UNITRATE);
   printf("Standing charge       £%7.2f\n\n", STANDCHARGE);
   printf("The sum due is        £%7.2f\n",
          (present-previous)*UNITRATE/100 + STANDCHARGE);
   printf(ASTERISKS);

}
```

In Program 1.7, the two values, standing charge and unit rate, will be the same each time the program is obeyed, over a fairly long period. Firstly, giving names to these values makes the program more readable. Secondly, if at some future date electricity prices rise, we can change the values of standing charge and unit rate very easily. Only the constant definition needs to be changed. Otherwise we would have to change the appropriate values wherever they had been written into the text of the program. In a longer program, standing charge and unit rate may have been used a large number of times.

In Program 1.7 there are three named constants in use, and they are defined separately. One of these, ASTERISKS, is a **string** constant.

The names of constants are usually typed entirely in capitals by convention, so that they can be easily distinguished from variables.

1.7 ■ Testing and debugging

As we mentioned in the Introduction, we cannot assume that programs are always written correctly and then keyed into the computer without any mistakes. Variables may not be declared; they may be declared to be the wrong type; the wrong formatting codes may be used in scanf statements, and so on. At the typing stage, characters or even whole lines may be omitted and extra characters may be inserted. The range of mistakes that can be made will increase with each chapter.

Finding errors can be difficult for a beginner, so at the end of each chapter we have presented a table of common programming problems, together with their symptoms.

The best way to debug a program that has errors is to arrange for the program to print out additional diagnostic information at the testing stage. To do this, additional printf statements can be inserted at key points in the program, after any suspect code. A typical debugging statement might be:

```
printf("After scanf, debt=%f\n", debt);
```

Once testing is complete and the programmer is satisfied that the program is correct, any debugging statements can be deleted, or, even better, they can be commented out in case they are needed again during future developments of the program:

```
/*printf("After scanf, debt=%f\n", debt);*/
```

At the end of each chapter, we have included some tips about inserting diagnostic print statements.

━━━━━━━━━━━━━ SUMMARY OF CHAPTER 1 ━━━━━━━━━━━━━

Key points

■ We can think of a **variable** as a named box in which a program can store something.

■ A scanf statement allows your program to get data from the user at the keyboard into a variable.

■ Integer variables can store whole numbers, and floating point variables are used to store numbers with a fractional part.

Good programming practice

■ Insert comments to make your programs easier to understand.

■ Use meaningful names for variables.

■ Use named constants to make your programs easier to read and easier to change.

Common problems	
Problem	**Symptom**
Missing semicolon.	Syntax error *at start of next statement*.
Missing or incorrect end-of-comment bracket (for example, space between * and /)	Everything up to the end of the next comment will be ignored, resulting in meaningless syntax error messages or strange run-time behaviour.
Missing & before variable in `scanf`.	Value read is placed somewhere else in the computer memory – this could destroy the contents of one of your variables or, more seriously, memory being used by other software on your computer. Program may behave oddly or computer may seize up completely.
Using `%i` to read into a `float` or `%f` to read into an `int`.	Unexpected values are placed in the variables concerned.
Using anything other than simple format codes such as `%i` or `%f` in `scanf` (for example, do not use `%4i`, `%.2f`, `\n`, or any spaces or punctuation in a formatting string).	Unexpected values are placed in the variables concerned.

Debugging tip

■ Place an extra `printf` to print values of variables immediately after any suspect `scanf` statements or suspect sections of program.

EXERCISES FOR CHAPTER 1

(1) Write a program that accepts as input a person's current bank balance and the amount of a withdrawal. The program should display the new balance.

(2) A student has taken four examination papers. Write a program that reads her four marks (integers) and displays her average mark.

(3) A pay rise of 12.5% has been awarded to a company's employees and is to be backdated for seven months. Write a program to which an employee can supply as input his previous annual salary and which will inform him how much additional back-dated pay he should receive.

(4) When a company's employee retires, she will be entitled to an annual pension of one fiftieth of her current annual salary for each complete year's service with the company. Write a program into which she can type her current annual salary and the number of complete years she has served with the company. The program should inform her what her annual pension should be.

(5) Write a program that reads two integers and reports their sum and product in the form of two equations.

For example, if the input is:

```
4 7
```

the output should be:

```
4 + 7 = 11
4 * 7 = 28
```

(6) Write a program that reads the gross price of an item sold and a discount rate (as a percentage). The program should display a sales invoice, for example:

```
***********************
gross price      $56.25
discount rate     2.5%      - two decimal places
discount         $ 1.41       between 0-100
discount price   $54.84
***********************
```

(A percentage sign can be printed by a `printf` statement by including `%%` in the formatting string.)

(7) Write a program that reads a standard hourly rate of pay, number of ordinary hours worked and number of overtime hours worked. The overtime rate is 1.5 times the standard rate. Write a program that displays a payslip for the employee concerned.

(8) Write a program that draws a Christmas tree outline using asterisks and displays the message 'a merry Christmas' in the centre of the tree.

(9) Write a program that displays your first initial in the form of a letter several lines high; for example:

```
    JJ
    JJ
    JJ
JJ  JJ
JJJJJJ
 JJJJ
```

(10) Write a program that reads a person's income for a year and his or her total tax
allowance. No income tax is to be paid on the amount earned up to the tax
allowance. All remaining income is to be taxed at a standard rate of 25%. The program should print a tax bill. (Assume that the income is greater than the tax
allowance.)

Rate of howly pay

\# of regular howers worked

\# of overtime hows worked

reg pay

overtime pay

total pay

rate of pay 2 decimal places

hours worked 2 decimal

Salary $ ____

Hours   Rate   Earnings

Regular

O.T

Total

CHAPTER 2

Doing calculations

Doing arithmetic calculations is one of the functions frequently performed by a computer. This chapter tells you more about how to write instructions to make the computer do arithmetic.

2.1 ■ Assignment statements

As we have seen, to put a value or number into a variable we can write:

```
scanf("%i", &m);
```

If the value 3 is supplied as input when the program is obeyed, this value is placed in the variable named m:

m [3]

The statement:

```
m = 3;
```

also places 3 in the variable m. This is known as an **assignment** statement because it assigns a value to the variable. The symbol '=' should be read as 'becomes equal to'. The left-hand side of an assignment statement must be the name of a variable to which the right-hand side is to be assigned. In the simplest cases, the right-hand side can be a constant, as in the above example, or another variable name:

```
m = n;
```

In this example the contents of n are put into m (the previous contents of m being destroyed or overwritten).

Thus, if before the statement is obeyed we have:

m [2]   n [3]

after the statement is obeyed we have:

m ③   n ③

Note that the value in n is left unchanged. We do not *take out* the value in n, but *copy* it into m.

2.2 ▤ The use of simple arithmetic expressions

The right-hand side of an assignment statement can in fact be any expression similar to those we have used so far in printf statements; for example:

```
i = j + k;
```

If before the above statement is obeyed we have:

i ③   j ④   k ⑤

then immediately after the statement is obeyed we have:

i ⑨   j ④   k ⑤

Note that a statement such as:

```
x = x + y;
```

which, if you are used to algebraic equations, may seem somewhat peculiar, is perfectly valid and means: the value of x becomes equal to what it was before plus the value of y. The right-hand side of an assignment statement is always evaluated first, regardless of what variable appears on the left.

Thus, if we have:

x 3.1   y 4.2

then immediately after the above statement is obeyed we have:

x 7.3   y 4.2

Now consider part of a program that finds the sum and average of three numbers:

```
scanf("%f%f%f", &x, &y, &z);
printf("The sum is: %f. The average is: %f.\n", x+y+z, (x+y+z)/3);
```

This would be better written as:

```
scanf("%f%f%f", &x, &y, &z);
sum = x + y + z;
printf("The sum is: %f. The average is: %f.\n", sum, sum/3);
```

In the second version the expression x + y + z is evaluated only once instead of twice, and the second version is easier to read. As the programs you write get more complicated you should tend to organize them in this way. In this case we could also have written:

```
x = x + y + z;
```

and avoided using the extra variable sum. However, this would detract from the readability of the program, as well as destroying the contents of one of the original variables.

Program 2.1 is another version of the room size program, which makes use of extra variables perimeter and FloorArea to hold the values of arithmetic expressions that would otherwise be recalculated.

PROGRAM 2.1

This program calculates the perimeter, wall area, floor area and volume of a room, given its dimensions.

```
/* Program 2.1 : Room Size 3 */

#include <stdio.h>

void main (void)
{
   float length, width, height, perimeter, FloorArea;

   printf("Type in length, width and height of room:\n");
   scanf("%f%f%f", &length, &width, &height);

   perimeter = 2*(length+width);
   FloorArea = length*width;
   printf("Skirting board: %.2f m.\n", perimeter);
   printf("Wall paper: %.2f sq.m.\n", perimeter*height);
   printf("Carpet: %.2f sq.m.\n", FloorArea);
   printf("Fresh air: %.2f cu.m.\n", FloorArea*height);

}
```

2.3 ■ Some alternative syntax

C provides abbreviated notations for many forms of assignment statement. Some programmers make extensive use of these, and you will need to be familiar with them. However, such abbreviations can obscure the meaning of a program, and many of the more complex uses of abbreviations are best avoided. In this book, we shall use only simple examples whose meanings are clear.

We have seen statements such as:

```
size = size + 3;
```

This can also be written in C as:

```
size += 3;
```

which saves on typing, especially if the variable name is long. Similarly, the statements:

```
x = x * 3;
y = y / 4;
z = z - 5;
```

can be rewritten as:

```
x *= 3;
y /= 4;
z -= 5;
```

And in the special case where we are adding the value 1 to a variable, instead of the statement:

```
count = count + 1;
```

or

```
count += 1;
```

we can simply write:

```
count++;
```

To reduce the value of the variable by 1 we can use:

```
count--;
```

All of the above operators, and indeed the assignment operator itself, can unfortunately be used freely in building up expressions in C. For example, you might see statements such as:

```
n = 2*(i++)*(j++)/(m=2);
```

which not only assigns a new value to n, but also has the side effects of giving new values to i, j and m. Using any of these operators on the right-hand side of an assignment is highly dangerous (except in very simple cases) and we suggest that you do not attempt to do it!

2.4 ■ More about arithmetic expressions: Order of evaluation

In the arithmetic expressions used so far, we have sometimes used parentheses. For example:

```
average = (x + y + z)/3;
```

or

```
perimeter = 2*(length + width);
```

In each case we have used the parentheses to clarify our intentions. We want the computer to calculate:

$$\frac{x+y+z}{3}$$

so we write:

```
(x + y + z)/3
```

This is simply a consequence of the fact that we are using a keyboard, and arithmetic expressions must be typed as a sequence of characters, one after another.

If we missed out the parentheses:

```
average = x + y + z/3;
```

the computer would calculate:

$$x+y+\frac{z}{3}$$

which is not what we intended.

In the other example, if we removed the parentheses:

```
perimeter = 2*length + width;
```

the computer would calculate:

```
(2*length) + width
```

You can see from this that the computer has rules for dealing with the evaluation of arithmetic expressions.

Let us begin by listing the **arithmetic operators** that have been informally introduced so far:

```
+ addition
- subtraction
* multiplication
/ division
```

The computer can perform only one of these operations at a time. To perform an operation it requires two **operands**, which are the quantities on either side of the operator. In the absence of parentheses, multiplication and division are carried out before addition and subtraction.

Consider the expression:

```
a/b + c/d*e
```

The computer evaluates this as follows (Figure 2.1):

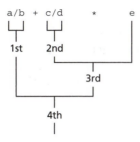

Figure 2.1 The computer carries out an operation according to a particular order of evaluation.

- first result evaluated: a/b
- second result evaluated: c/d
- third result evaluated: second result * e
- fourth result evaluated: first result + third result

Thus, the computer evaluates:

$$\frac{a}{b} + \frac{c}{d} * e$$

If instead we wanted the computer to evaluate:

$$\frac{a}{b} + \frac{c}{d * e}$$

then we would use parentheses as follows:

a/b + c/(d*e)

Anything inside parentheses is evaluated first. For the operators introduced so far, we can summarize this order of **precedence**, as it is called, as follows:

- first: anything inside parentheses
- second: multiplication and division
- third: addition and subtraction

In this list, adjacent operators of the same precedence are applied from left to right.

Programs 2.2 and 2.3 illustrate two solutions to the same problem. These programs do calculations involving times of day. For now, we express a time as a floating point number of hours after midnight. We shall see later in this chapter how to handle input and output of times in hours-and-minutes form.

Program 2.3 is a more 'efficient' version of Program 2.2. Efficiency in this context means that this program, which has an effect identical to that of Program 2.2, involves fewer arithmetic calculations and uses fewer variables.

Program 2.2 involves six additions and three divisions, whereas Program 2.3 involves three additions and three divisions. Any time saving will be tiny, but when an operation is repeated millions of times in a large program, this sort of consideration becomes more important.

Instead of using the three variables TimeAt1, TimeAt2 and TimeAt3, Program 2.3 uses a single variable that gets bigger and bigger as the program is obeyed. At each step, we are saying: TimeSoFar becomes equal to its previous value plus the new time interval. This idea becomes important later on, when loops that process more than three values are introduced.

PROGRAM 2.2

This program reads into the three variables dist1, dist2 and dist3 the three distances between four towns along a railway line. Given a start time and an average speed in m.p.h. the program displays the time of arrival at each town (assuming that stopping time is negligible). Times are expressed as a floating point number of hours after midnight; for example 8.75 means 08.45 a.m. We assume that the journey takes place all on one day.

```
/* Program 2.2 : Times */

#include <stdio.h>

void main (void)
{
   float dist1, dist2, dist3, mph;
   float StartTime, TimeAt1, TimeAt2, TimeAt3;

   printf("3 distances:");   scanf("%f%f%f", &dist1, &dist2, &dist3);
   printf("Start time:");    scanf("%f", &StartTime);
   printf("Average speed:");scanf("%f", &mph);

   TimeAt1 = StartTime + dist1/mph;
   printf("Time of arrival at town 1 is %4.2f\n", TimeAt1);

   TimeAt2 = StartTime + (dist1+dist2)/mph;
   printf("Time of arrival at town 2 is %4.2f\n", TimeAt2);

   TimeAt3 = StartTime + (dist1+dist2+dist3)/mph;
   printf("Time of arrival at town 3 is %4.2f\n", TimeAt3);

}
```

━━━━━━━━━━━━━━ **PROGRAM 2.3** ━━━━━━━━━━━━━━

This is a variation on Program 2.2.

```
/* Program 2.3 : Times 2 */

#include <stdio.h>

void main(void)
{
    float dist1, dist2, dist3, mph, StartTime, TimeSoFar;

    printf("3 distances:");   scanf("%f%f%f", &dist1, &dist2, &dist3);
    printf("Start time:");    scanf("%f", &StartTime);
    printf("Average speed:");scanf("%f", &mph);

    TimeSoFar = StartTime + dist1/mph;
    printf("Time of arrival at town 1 is %4.2f\n", TimeSoFar);

    TimeSoFar = TimeSoFar + dist2/mph;
    printf("Time of arrival at town 2 is %4.2f\n", TimeSoFar);

    TimeSoFar = TimeSoFar + dist3/mph;
    printf("Time of arrival at town 3 is %4.2f\n", TimeSoFar);

}
```

2.5 ■ Integer operators

In the two previous examples, we used the division operator, /, on floating point values to produce another floating point value. In both examples, division was only ever performed using floating point values. In fact, it can also be used to divide an integer by a floating point number, or vice versa, again producing a floating point result.

However, when the / operator is used on two integers, the result is *not* a floating point value. Dividing an integer by an integer will produce an integer result – if the division is not exact, the remainder is discarded.

The / operator used on two integers in this way has a counterpart, the % operator (not to be confused with the % formatting codes used in printf and scanf). This operator is used on two integers to provide an integer result – the remainder after the two numbers are divided. The % operator has the same precedence as / and *.

Consider the following examples:

Expression	Value
16.0 / 5.0	3.2
16 / 5	3
16 % 5	1
19.0 / 5	3.8
19 / 5	3
19 % 5	4
8 / 3 * 3	6
7 + 5 / 3	8
13 - 5 % 3	11

Program 2.4 illustrates a typical use of the integer operators.

PROGRAM 2.4

This is a supermarket 'checkout' program that displays the number and denomination of coins required to make up the change from £1 for a purchase costing less than £1 (a whole number of pennies). The program indicates the number of 50p, 20p, 10p, 5p, 2p and 1p coins to be paid out.

```
/* Program 2.4 : Change */

#include <stdio.h>

void main (void)
{
  int price, change,
      fifties, twenties, tens, fives, twos, ones;

  printf("\nPrice in pence(<100):");
  scanf("%i", &price);
  change = 100 - price;

  fifties = change / 50; change = change % 50;
  twenties = change / 20; change = change % 20;
  tens = change / 10; change = change % 10;
  fives = change  / 5;   change = change % 5;
  twos = change  / 2;   change = change % 2;
  ones = change;

  printf("Change due is:\n");
  printf("%i 50s, %i 20s, %i 10s, %i 5s, %i 2s and %i 1s.\n",
        fifties, twenties, tens, fives, twos, ones );
}
```

We have now introduced five arithmetic operators, one of which, %, can be applied only to integer quantities. A complete list of operators (some of which have not yet been introduced) is given in Appendix B.

2.6 ■ More about int and float variables

At this point some further notes on the differences between int and float variables are appropriate. You have already seen that we distinguish between variables that are going to contain integer numbers and variables that are going to contain floating point numbers. In general, you should ensure that int variables are used for values that can only be whole numbers and float variables are used for values that may have a fractional part.

The classification of a variable as int or float is called its **type**. In C there are several types we can use to classify variables. Up to now we have introduced only two basic types, but others will be introduced later.

The computer sometimes uses this type information to detect errors made by the programmer. For example, if you write

```
int a;
float x;
:
a = 15 % x;
```

the computer will inform you that you have made a type error and the program would not be run. In this example you have tried to apply the % operator with a floating point variable when two integers are expected.

Note that assignment *is* possible between variables of different types. For example:

```
int a;
float x;
a = 2;
:
x = a;
```

In this example, the value of x after assignment will be the floating point number 2.0.

The converse is also possible:

```
int a;
float x;
x = 2.74;
:
a = x;
```

In this case the value of a after assignment will be 2, since an int variable can hold only whole numbers – the fractional part is discarded and the number is **truncated**. When a floating point number is assigned to an integer, the number always moves towards zero. The following examples summarize the effect:

```
int a;
a =  2.74   /* a becomes   2 */
a =  2.24   /* a becomes   2 */
a = -2.74   /* a becomes  -2 */
a = -2.24   /* a becomes  -2 */
```

Information is lost when a floating point number is put into an integer variable – if you are not careful, an innocent looking assignment could lead to unexpected results. In general, it will be good programming practice to try to use only matching types in assignment statements. Occasionally, mixed type assignments will be useful, particularly for extracting the whole number part of a floating point value. Another useful trick that uses mixed type assignments allows us to round a *positive* floating point number to the *nearest* integer. If we add 0.5 to the floating point number and then truncate it using an assignment statement, the result will be the nearest integer. For example:

```
int a;
a = 2.74 + 0.5   /* a becomes 3 */
a = 2.24 + 0.5   /* a becomes 2 */
```

This method of rounding does not work for negative numbers, as you will see if you try some examples.

Occasionally, it is convenient to have a way of telling the computer to convert an int to a float without including an extra assignment. For example, if an int variable total is to be divided by an int count to produce a float average, we *cannot* use:

```
int total, count;
float average;
  ⋮
average = total / count;
```

This is because division of two integers gives an integer value and any fractional part is lost *before* the result is assigned to average and converted back to a floating point number. We must convert at least one of the integers to a floating point number before division takes place. We could do this by assigning one of them to a new float variable, but a neater way of doing it is to use an explicit **type cast**:

```
int total, count;
float average;
  ⋮
average = total / (float)count;
```

The appearance of (float) before an integer expression says that it should be converted to floating point representation before being included in the current calculation. In this case, this is sufficient to ensure that the division produces a floating point result. If we were dividing `total` by the constant value 3 to obtain a float, the 3 can be more easily converted to a floating point value:

```
average = total / 3.0;
```

This approach is used in Program 2.5, where an integer number of minutes is divided by 60.0 to convert it into a floating point number of hours.

PROGRAM 2.5

Given a distance between two towns, a speed in miles per hour and a departure time from one town, this program displays the arrival time at the other town. Times are input as, for example, 0845 or 1357 and are output as, for example, 8:45 and 13:57. We again assume that the journey takes place in one day.

```
/* Program 2.5 : Journey */

#include <stdio.h>

void main (void)
{
    int StartTime, hours, mins;
    float dist, mph, FloatHours;

    printf("Distance:");       scanf("%f", &dist);
    printf("Start time:");     scanf("%i", &StartTime);
    printf("Average speed:");  scanf("%f", &mph);

    hours = StartTime / 100;
    mins  = StartTime % 100;
    FloatHours = hours + mins/60.0;

        /* next statement calculates time of arrival */
        /* as a float number of hours after midnight  */
    FloatHours = FloatHours + dist/mph;

        /* time now converted back into minutes */
        /* rounded to nearest minute */
    mins = FloatHours*60 + 0.5;

        /* now convert minutes to hours and minutes */
    hours = mins/60;
    mins = mins % 60;
    printf("Arrival time: %2i:%02i\n", hours, mins);

}
```

Finally, you should remember that the computer stores integer numbers and floating point numbers in different ways. Although this is normally of little concern to the novice programmer, it does mean that the largest floating point number the computer can handle is much bigger than the largest integer number. As indicated in Chapter 1, the actual ranges may depend on your system, but `int` should allow whole numbers up to at least 32 767, and `float` should allow at least six digits of precision.

Let us now return to a problem raised by Program 2.2 and see how we can cope with expressing times such as 12.95 hours after midnight as 1257. One way of doing this is illustrated in Program 2.5.

Note the use of the format code `%02i` on the last `printf` statement in Program 2.5. This says that an integer should be printed occupying two character positions, and that zeros should be inserted, if necessary, rather than spaces. Thus, a time such as 11:03 is printed with the zero, rather than as 11: 3.

2.7 ■ The standard library

We first saw the line:

```
#include <stdio.h>
```

in the Introduction. This line is necessary to give your program access to functions related to input and output. The programs for evaluating these standard functions have already been written and are stored as part of your C system. There is a certain minimum set of functions that should be available with C, called the **standard library**. `stdio.h` is the name of a so-called **header file** that contains information about a group of functions from the standard library. Another such header file is `math.h`, which stores information about standard mathematics functions. To use these functions, our program should include the line:

```
#include <math.h>
```

along with any other `#include` lines required. The following examples use functions from `math.h`.

```
x = 4.0;
printf("%f\n", sqrt(x));
```

displays the value:

```
2.000000
```

and

```
y = 5.66;
printf("%f\n", floor(y));
```

displays the value

```
5.000000
```

sqrt is the name of the standard function that performs the operation 'finding the square root of'. floor is the name of the standard function that finds the whole number just below the floating point number to which we are applying it; that is, positive numbers get truncated to the whole number below (represented as a floating point value). Negative numbers are moved away from zero. To summarize:

```
int a;
a = floor( 2.74)   /* a becomes  2.0 */
a = floor( 2.24)   /* a becomes  2.0 */
a = floor(-2.74)   /* a becomes -3.0 */
a = floor(-2.24)   /* a becomes -3.0 */
```

When you refer to a function you use its name and enclose within parentheses the value to which the function is to be applied. This value, which is called a **parameter** or an **argument**, can be any arithmetic expression of a type appropriate for the particular function.

For example:

```
x = sqrt(16);
   ⋮
x = sqrt(y);
   ⋮
x = sqrt(3*y/z);
   ⋮
x = 15.6 + sqrt(3*y/z);
```

Because parameters can be arithmetic expressions, a function can be used in an expression that is the parameter of another function:

```
printf("%f\n", floor(sqrt(17.3)) );
```

displays 4.000000, and:

```
printf("%f\n", sqrt(sqrt(16)) );
```

displays 2.000000, and:

```
theta = 3.142/3;
printf("%f\n", sqrt(sin(theta) + cos(theta)) );
```

displays 1.168750.

You must ensure that the parameter given to a function, whether it is a constant, a variable or an expression, is of an appropriate type. However, as the second of these three examples shows, it is possible to pass an integer to a function that generally expects a floating point value. In the same way that int values and float values were compatible in assignment (Section 2.6), the integer 16 is passed as the floating point value 16.0.

There is a list of some of the commonly used standard functions in Appendix C, together with information on the types of parameters required and the types of results produced.

Program 2.6 illustrates the use of the cos function. If you are not familiar with the trigonometry involved in this example, do not worry – just skip over it. You should note that while people usually work in degrees, the parameters of trigonometric functions in the standard library have to be given in radians, hence the conversion in this program.

PROGRAM 2.6

For a standard 'inverted v' shaped roof, this program works out the area of roof covering required, given the length and width of the building and the angular pitch in degrees of the roof (Figure 2.2).

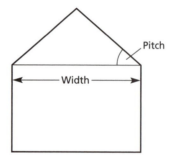

Figure 2.2 Measurements required to calculate roof area.

```c
/* Program 2.6 : Roof */
#include <stdio.h>
#include <math.h>
void main (void)
{
   float pitch, length, width, AreaOfRoof;
   printf("Type in pitch of roof (degrees), length and width:\n");
   scanf("%f%f%f", &pitch, &length, &width);
   pitch = pitch * 3.14159/180;
   AreaOfRoof = width / cos(pitch) * length;
  printf("Area of roof is %f sq.m.\n", AreaOfRoof);

}
```

Program 2.7 illustrates the use of the pow function, which raises a number to a power. pow is a standard function that takes *two* parameters.

===== **PROGRAM 2.7** =====

This program uses the pow function (raise a number to a power) from math.h to find the surface area and volume of a cube.

```
/* Program 2.7 : Powers */

#include <stdio.h>
#include <math.h>

void main (void)
{
   float edge, surface, volume;

   printf("Length of edge?\n");
   scanf("%f", &edge);

   surface = 6 * pow(edge, 2);
   volume  = pow(edge, 3);
   printf("Surface area is %.2f, volume is %.2f\n",
                                      surface, volume);

}
```

===== **SUMMARY OF CHAPTER 2** =====

Key points

■ In this chapter you learned to assign a value to a variable; for example:

   x = 1;

■ An entire expression is evaluated by evaluating subexpressions in a specific sequence depending on the operators involved. Each operator has an **order of precedence**, which is used to determine which subexpression should be evaluated first.

■ Parentheses (round brackets) can be used to explicitly change the order of evaluation.

■ The **integer** operators % and / have the same precedence as the familiar operations of multiplication and division.

■ Functions from the **standard library** can be used when the appropriate header file is included at the start of your program. For example, the mathematical functions floor, sqrt, sin, cos and pow are all available when the header file math.h is included.

Good programming practice

- If you find yourself calculating the same result twice, calculate it once, storing the result in a variable.
- Avoid the many abbreviations provided by C where they obscure meaning.
- Try to use only matching types in assignment statements, except for deliberately rounding or truncating a `float` to an `int`.

Common problems	
Problem	**Symptom**
Mismatched brackets in expression.	Syntax errors at the end of the expression.
Wrongly placed or missing brackets in expression, for example `x/y*z` instead of `x/(y*z)`.	Wrong values calculated. If in doubt, put in extra brackets to make the intended meaning clear. This is a common mistake when using a calculator to evaluate an expression.
Inadvertent use of integer division, for example `1/3` is `0` and `i/3` is truncated if `i` is an integer. This applies even within a larger expression, so that `26.5*(1/3)` is `0.0`.	Wrong values calculated.
Division by zero.	A run-time floating point error message.

Debugging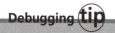

- Place an extra `printf` to print values of variables after suspect assignment statements.

EXERCISES FOR CHAPTER 2

(1) A pay rise of 9.9% has been awarded to a company's employees. Write a program to which an employee can supply as input his previous annual salary and which will inform him of his new annual, monthly and weekly rates of pay. (Assume that there are exactly 52 weeks in the year.)

(2) A sum of money has been invested at an annual rate of interest of 14.75%. Interest is calculated and added to the account at the end of each complete year. Write a program that reads the initial amount invested and displays the balance in the account at the end of each of the first three years.

(3) A retiring employee is entitled to an annual pension of one fiftieth of his current annual salary for each complete year's service with the company. All employees start work on the first day of a month and retire on the last day of a month. Write a program into which an employee can type his current annual salary, the month and year he started work with the company, and the month and year he retired. (A month is supplied as an integer in the range 1–12.) The program should inform the employee what his annual pension will be.

➡ **Hint**: Calculate the total number of months worked and use integer division to find the number of complete years worked.

(4) A car hire company calculates the charge for the hire of a car using a standard rate for each mile travelled together with a 'wear and tear' surcharge for each complete 1000 miles travelled. Write a program that accepts as input the milometer readings at the start and finish of a hire and calculates the total charge for the hire.

(5) The floor of a room is to be covered with tiles of dimension 15 cm square. There is to be a gap of 2 mm between tiles when laid. Write a program that, given the room dimensions (in metres), works out the number of whole tiles required. (Calculation of the number of extra tiles required for cutting is somewhat tricky and is left for a later chapter.)

(6) Write a program that accepts as input the amount of cash (a floating point number of pounds or dollars) to be enclosed in an employee's pay packet. The program should do a 'coin and note analysis' and display the number of coins and notes, of each available denomination, which are to be included in the pay packet.

➡ **Hint**: Separate the cash amount into pounds and pence, or dollars and cents, using something like the following:

```
int pounds,pence; float pay;
    .
    .
    .
pounds = pay;
pence  =  (pay-pounds)*100 + 0.5;
```

Note that the +0.5 is essential, otherwise a penny or a cent will occasionally be lost because of rounding errors that can take place during the calculations. Then deal separately with the two amounts as illustrated in Program 2.4.

(7) Given a departure and arrival time based on the 24-hour clock and input as in Program 2.5, write a program that will display the duration in hours and minutes of the journey (assumed to take place all in one day).

Now assume that the departure and arrival times are quoted according to two different time zones, and modify the program to accept a third input that is a positive or negative time margin (a whole number of hours), which is to be applied to the arrival time before doing the above calculation. (Again assume that no change of day takes place.)

CHAPTER 3

Selecting alternatives

Here we encounter our first **control statements**. A control statement determines what parts of a program should be executed and in what order. In this chapter, we introduce the conditional statements that give computers much of their flexibility – the ability to make tests while a program is running and choose alternative courses of action based on the results of these tests.

3.1 ■ Simple `if` statements

Here we look at how we can tell the computer to select one of two alternatives. In the first instance we consider that one of the alternatives is to do nothing. A statement is either obeyed or ignored, depending on the outcome of a test.

Consider the following simple examples:

```
if (age > 18)
  printf("Eligible for jury service.\n");

if (CigarettesPerDay > 5)
  printf("Cut down on smoking.\n");

if (PreviousConvictions > 3)
  fine = fine * 2;

if (SaleTotal > 100)
  SaleTotal = 0.9 * SaleTotal;
```

In each of these examples the form is:

if (condition)
  statement;

A simple condition relates two quantities using one of a number of relational operators. The particular relational operator we used above was >, which means 'greater than'.

Note the use of additional spaces at the start of the second line in each of the above examples. This makes the subsidiary part of the if statement stand out from the surrounding text, and the use of such **indentation** can make complex programs much more readable than they would otherwise be.

The complete list of relational operators is:

Operator	Meaning
>	greater than
>=	greater than or equal to
<	less than
<=	less than or equal to
==	equal to
!=	not equal to

The operators >=, <= and != are single operators, written in this way because of the limited number of characters usually available on a keyboard. The following examples use these operators:

```
if (age >= 18)
  printf("Eligible for jury service.\n");

if (i != j)
  printf("i and j are unequal.\n");
```

In general, floating point numbers should *not* be compared using == or !=. Two values that we think should be identical may differ very slightly when represented inside the computer. Although numbers are represented in binary form inside the computer, the problem can be illustrated easily using decimal numbers.

If we try to write the value of the expression 1.0/3.0 as a decimal fraction, we must truncate the repeating digits at some point and write it as, for example, 0.333333. The result of the calculation 1.0/3.0*3.0 done using this notation would therefore be 0.999999, which is not exactly equal to 1. Exactly the same problem arises using a binary representation of fractions. So after the sequence of statements:

```
x = 1.0;
y = x/3.0;
z = y*3.0;
if (x==z) ...
```

the result of the test would certainly be false. Because we are not familiar with the binary arithmetic which is being used behind the scenes by the computer, similar problems arise even in unexpected places, and we should always ask whether two

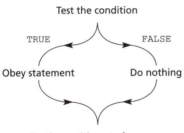

Test the condition

TRUE   FALSE

Obey statement   Do nothing

Continue with rest of program

Figure 3.1 The behaviour of a simple `if` statement.

floating point numbers are very close to each other, rather than equal. For example, in the above case we should test whether x and z are close by using:

```
if (fabs(x-z) < 0.0001)
    printf("x and z are almost equal.\n");
```

where `fabs` is a standard function from `math.h` that finds the absolute value of a floating point number. The absolute value of a number is its size (that is, without the minus sign if it is negative). We need to use `fabs` here as we do not usually know which of the two numbers being tested is bigger.

The behaviour of a simple `if` statement can be illustrated as shown in Figure 3.1. The branch taken depends on the outcome of the test. If the condition is satisfied, then the left-hand branch is followed; otherwise, the right-hand branch is taken. We say that the outcome of a test is TRUE or FALSE, and this is a concept of which we shall make frequent use later.

You must *not* put a semicolon after `if (condition)` because this will completely change the meaning of the `if` statement. Your program will still run, but the statement to be obeyed or ignored is simply the so-called **empty statement**. Thus, for example:

```
if (SaleTotal > 100);
    SaleTotal = 0.9 * SaleTotal;
```

will not have the expected effect. Because of the semicolon at the end of the first line, the statement on the second line will always be obeyed, regardless of the result of the test. If this erroneous `if` statement appeared in the middle of a large program, the error could go unnoticed – a discount of 10% would be given for sales that were ineligible for a discount. The careless programmer would not be popular with the management!

Program 3.1 illustrates the use of simple `if` statements.

PROGRAM 3.1

Four numbers are input to this program. The first number is interpreted as a standard value and the three further values are compared with this standard value. A message is printed indicating how many of these three values are within 0.1 of the standard value.

```
/* Program 3.1 : Tolerance */

#include <stdio.h>
#include <math.h>

void main(void)
{
   float standard, next; int NumberClose;
   NumberClose = 0;
   printf("Standard value?");  scanf("%f", &standard);

   printf("next test value?");  scanf("%f", &next);
   if (fabs(standard - next) < 0.1) NumberClose++;

   printf("next test value?");  scanf("%f", &next);
   if (fabs(standard - next) < 0.1) NumberClose++;

   printf("next test value?");  scanf("%f", &next);
   if (fabs(standard - next) < 0.1) NumberClose++;

   printf("%i", NumberClose);
   printf(" values are near the standard.\n");

}
```

For example, if the values input (in response to the prompts) are:

```
3.156  3.051  3.152  3.091
```

the output will be:

```
2 values are near the standard.
```

In Program 3.1 the same operations are being performed three times over. A more elegant way of writing this program, particularly if more values were being compared, would be to put the repeated statements inside a loop. We shall introduce such loops in subsequent chapters.

3.2 ■ **Simple** `if-else` **statements**

Now consider the following examples:

```
if (age > 18)
   printf("Eligible for jury service.\n");
else
   printf("Under age; not eligible for jury service.\n");

if (AlcoholUnitsPerWeek > 21)
   printf("Cut down on your drinking.\n");
else
   printf("Alcohol consumption is within recommended limits.\n");

if (SaleTotal > 100)
   SaleTotal = 0.9 * SaleTotal;
else
   SaleTotal = 0.95 * SaleTotal;

if (age > 60)
   benefit = (age-60)*annualrate;
else
   printf("No benefit payable.\n");

if (CurrentReading > PreviousReading)
   unitsused = CurrentReading - PreviousReading;
else
   unitsused = 10000 - PreviousReading + CurrentReading;

if (i != j)
   printf("i and j are unequal.\n");
else
   printf("i and j are equal.\n");
```

In each of the above examples the general form is:

> *if (condition)*
>   *statement1;*
> *else*
>   *statement2;*

The behaviour of a simple `if-else` statement can be illustrated as shown in Figure 3.2. Again, we are selecting one out of two alternatives but this time the second alternative, instead of being to do nothing, is another statement. Again, the selection

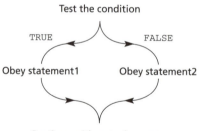

Continue with rest of program

Figure 3.2 The behaviour of a simple `if-else` statement.

is dependent on the outcome of the test, which can be either TRUE or FALSE. Technically, we say that the condition has a **value** TRUE or FALSE. Statement1 is executed if (the value of) the condition is TRUE, otherwise statement2 is executed because (the value of) the condition is FALSE.

A similar warning about the careless use of semicolons applies to `if-else` statements. No semicolon should appear after the `if (condition)` or after the `else`. A semicolon after the `if (condition)` would cause a syntax error message – the computer would think that the `if` statement had terminated and would not be able to make sense of the `else` when encountered. A semicolon after the `else` would still allow the program to run, but with errors in the results. For example:

```
if (SaleTotal > 100)
   SaleTotal = 0.9 * SaleTotal;
else;
   SaleTotal = 0.95 * SaleTotal;
```

The intention here is to give a 10% discount on sales over 100 and only a 5% discount on other sales. Because of the semicolon after the `else`, the alternative after the `else` is the empty statement. Thus, for a sale total over 100, the 10% discount adjustment will be made, and the **empty statement** after the `else` will be ignored. The statement that should have been ignored will then be obeyed and a further 5% discount will be given as well!

Programs 3.2 and 3.3 illustrate the use of `if-else` statements.

3.3 ■ The use of compound statements

It may be that the action to be selected according to the outcome of a test comprises a number of statements rather than a single statement. In this case such statements are bracketed together using braces {...}, as illustrated in Programs 3.4 and 3.5.

━━━━━━━━━ **PROGRAM 3.2** ━━━━━━━━━

This program reads three numbers and prints the largest.

```
/* Program 3.2 : Largest */
#include <stdio.h>
void main(void)
{
  float first, second, third, LargestSoFar, largest;
  printf("Enter three numbers:");
  scanf("%f%f%f", &first, &second, &third);
  if (first > second)
    LargestSoFar = first;
  else
    LargestSoFar = second;
  if (LargestSoFar > third)
    largest = LargestSoFar;
  else
    largest = third;
  printf("The largest number is: %.2f\n", largest);
}
```

━━━━━━━━━ **PROGRAM 3.3** ━━━━━━━━━

This program is similar to Program 1.3 except that if the payment is greater than the outstanding debt an appropriate message, together with a refund amount, is printed.

```
/* Program 3.3 : Loan Repayment */
#include <stdio.h>
#include <math.h>
void main (void)
{
  float debt, MonthlyRate, payment;
  printf("debt?");   scanf("%f", &debt);
  printf("monthly rate?");   scanf("%f", &MonthlyRate);
  printf("repayment?");   scanf("%f", &payment);
  debt = debt + debt*MonthlyRate/100 - payment;
  if (debt < 0)
    printf("Debt cleared. Refund = %.2f\n", -debt);
  else
    printf("Debt after this payment is %.2f\n", debt);
}
```

PROGRAM 3.4

This program finds the sum and difference of two numbers, ensuring that the larger of the two numbers ends up in the variable `larger` and the smaller in the variable `smaller`. Here we read the two numbers directly into the variables `larger` and `smaller` and swap the contents of these variables if necessary.

```
/* Program 3.4 : Two Numbers */

#include <stdio.h>

void main(void)
{
   int larger, smaller, temporary, sum, difference;
   printf("Enter two whole numbers:");
   scanf("%i%i", &larger, &smaller);

   if (larger < smaller)
   {
      temporary = larger;
      larger = smaller;
      smaller = temporary;
   }

   sum        = larger + smaller;
   difference = larger - smaller;

   printf("\n\nThe sum is %i\n", sum);
   printf("The difference is %i\n", difference);
   printf("Numbers in order are %i, %i\n", smaller, larger);
}
```

In the `if` statement of Program 3.4, the action to be performed if the outcome of the test is TRUE now consists of three statements bracketed together by {...} to form a single block. In this type of context, blocks are often referred to as **compound statements**. You should ensure that you understand the role played by the braces by considering what would happen if they were omitted:

```
if (larger < smaller)
   temporary = larger;
   larger = smaller;
   smaller = temporary;
```

In this case, only the single statement `temporary = larger;` is part of the `if` statement. The indentation at the start of the other two lines has no effect on the meaning of the program. If the condition is FALSE, only that one statement will be ignored and the next two will be obeyed inappropriately – `larger` will be set to the

━━━━━━━━━━━━━ **PROGRAM 3.5** ━━━━━━━━━━━━━

This program finds the sum and difference of two numbers as in Program 3.4. In this case, the two numbers are read initially into variables `first` and `second` and transferred into variables `larger` and `smaller` in the appropriate order.

```c
/* Program 3.5 : Two Numbers */
#include <stdio.h>
void main(void)
{
   int first, second, larger, smaller, sum, difference;
   printf("Enter two whole numbers:");
   scanf("%i%i", &first, &second);
   if (first < second)
   {
      smaller = first;
      larger  = second;
   }
   else
   {
      smaller = second;
      larger  = first;
   }
   sum        = larger + smaller;
   difference = larger - smaller;
   printf("\n\nThe sum is %i\n", sum);
   printf("The difference is %i\n", difference);
   printf("Numbers in order are %i, %i\n", smaller, larger);
}
```

value of `smaller` and `smaller` will have the contents of an undefined variable copied into it. Indentation should always be used to make programs more readable, but you should remember that it has no effect on the meaning of the program.

In order to swap over the contents of two variables, we need three assignment statements and one extra variable. You should examine what would happen if we had written:

```c
{
   larger = smaller;
   smaller = larger;
}
```

The same warnings given earlier about semicolons after the `if` `(condition)` and after the `else` still apply when using compound statements.

3.4 ■ More complicated conditions

The simple conditions we have used so far have been composed of two quantities related by a relational operator:

quantity1		relational operator		quantity2

The quantities we have used have been variables and constants, but they can also be arithmetic expressions:

```
if (sum1 + sum2 - credit > 250)
    printf("Limit exceeded.\n");

if (age - 60 < 5)
    benefit = LumpSum * 1.5;
else
    benefit = LumpSum;

if (total > 1.5 * CurrentBalance)
    printf("Limit exceeded.\n");
```

We can combine more than one condition in an `if` statement by joining conditions together using the operators `&&` and `||`. The first of these (`&&`) means 'and', and the second (`||`) means 'or'.

Consider the following examples:

```
if ((PreviousConvictions > 3) && (TimeSpread < 1.5))
    fine = fine * 4;

if ((weight > 200) && (height < 1.7))
    printf("You are overweight.\n");
else
    printf("Your weight is reasonable.\n");

if ((weight > 200) || (DailyCalories > 2000))
    printf("Cut down on eating.\n");
else
    printf("OK\n");

if ((x == y) && (x > 0) && (y > 0))
    printf("x and y are equal and positive.\n");
```

Individual conditions involving relational operators need not be enclosed in parentheses, but we will always do this because it makes the more complex conditions much more readable. The logical operators && and || join individual conditions together to make a more complex condition, in just the same way that arithmetic operators join arithmetic expressions together.

A common mistake made by new programmers is to write:

```
if (x > 0 && < 10)...
```

or

```
if (0 < x < 10)...
```

instead of:

```
if ((0 < x) && (x < 10))...
```

You should see from this that each constituent simple condition involving a relational operator must be complete.

3.5 ■ Definition of the logical operators

When an if statement contains a condition involving && and ||, the meaning of the condition is usually clear from reading the program. However, for completeness, here we tabulate the possible values of a composite condition involving two subsidiary conditions.

```
if (condition1 && condition2)......
```

Condition1	Condition2	Composite condition
FALSE	FALSE	FALSE
FALSE	TRUE	FALSE
TRUE	FALSE	FALSE
TRUE	TRUE	TRUE

```
if (condition1 || condition2)......
```

Condition1	Condition2	Composite condition
FALSE	FALSE	FALSE
FALSE	TRUE	TRUE
TRUE	FALSE	TRUE
TRUE	TRUE	TRUE

Note that the definition of 'or' used in mathematics and computing is the **inclusive** or – it includes as true the case where both subconditions are true. This contrasts with the 'or' used in day to day speech where, for example, telling a child that he or she can have 'a cake *or* a biscuit' does not usually include the alternative of having both.

Try making up your own examples using combinations of && and ||. The logical operators are often called boolean operators and conditions are often called boolean expressions after George Boole, the 19th-century English mathematician who developed the algebra of such expressions.

The other logical operator we use is !, which should be read as 'not'. Its use can be illustrated by a simple example:

```
if (!(x == y))
   printf("x and y are unequal.\n");
```

is exactly equivalent to:

```
if (x != y)
   printf("x and y are unequal.\n");
```

As with arithmetic operators, there is an order of precedence for logical operators. The order of precedence is ! then && then ||. Thus:

```
if ((calories > 2000) || (weight > 200) && (height < 1.7))
   printf("You are overeating.\n");
```

is equivalent to:

```
if ( (calories > 2000) || ((weight > 200) && (height < 1.7)) )
   printf("You are overeating.\n");
```

Remember, if in doubt, use extra parentheses to make your intentions clear.

Program 3.6 illustrates the use of the && operator. The if statement could have been rewritten using || as:

```
if ( (age < 18) || (age > 70) )
   printf("Not eligible for jury service.\n");
else
   printf("Eligible for jury service.\n");
```

3.6 ■ Logical values and variables

Earlier we said that the value of a logical expression is either TRUE or FALSE. Actually, from C's point of view, the value of a logical expression is an integer value which can be interpreted as TRUE or FALSE. C interprets the integer 0 as FALSE, and any other (that is, non-zero) integer as TRUE. So an integer variable can be used to store the value of a logical expression.

An integer variable in which we are going to store logical values can be declared just like any other integer variable:

```
int heavy, bright;
```

═══════════════ **PROGRAM 3.6** ═══════════════

In this program a person's age is read and a message printed that indicates whether the person is eligible for jury service or not.

```
/* Program 3.6 : Jury Service */

#include <stdio.h>

void main(void)
{
    int age;
    printf("What is your age?");
    scanf("%i", &age);

    if ( (age >= 18) && (age <= 70) )
        printf("Eligible for jury service.\n");
    else
        printf("Not eligible for jury service.\n");

}
```

For the purpose of clarity, when we assign a value to this variable, we shall use one of two constants defined as follows:

```
#define FALSE 0
#define TRUE 1
```

These definitions are standard, and will appear in one of the standard libraries with your C system, since they are used by some of the standard functions. For now, though, we will include them explicitly in any programs that require them. So, to assign values to our variables heavy and bright, we simply use, for example:

```
heavy = TRUE;
bright = FALSE;
```

If an integer variable is going to contain logical values, try to avoid using it to store other integers. Treat it as if it were a variable of a special type 'logical' which can only hold the two values TRUE and FALSE. This way you will avoid confusion.

The use of an integer variable to store a logical value is illustrated by the following fragment of program that prints out part of a menu. The dishes listed on the menu are to vary according to whether or not it is a summer month.

```
void main(void)
{
  int month;
  int ItsASummerMonth;

  printf("Month number for dinner party?");
  scanf("%i", &month);
  ItsASummerMonth = (month >= 5) && (month <= 8);
  printf("\n\n...Menu...\n\n");

  if (ItsASummerMonth)
    printf("Melon\n");
  else
    printf("Oysters\n");
  printf("\n");

  printf("Roast chicken with ");
  if (ItsASummerMonth)
    printf("green salad.\n");
  else
    printf("spuds and carrots.\n");
    ⋮
```

When the program is being obeyed, the value of the condition:

```
(month >= 5) && (month <= 8)
```

is TRUE or FALSE. This value is stored in the integer variable ItsASummerMonth. The program can then refer to the value of the condition as often as is necessary without having to perform the test again. The use of logical variables in examples like this can improve the readability or the efficiency of a program, particularly when the result of a test is to be used more than once. As another example, consider:

```
float height, weight; int tall, heavy;

scanf("%f%f", &height, &weight);
tall  = (height > 1.8);
heavy = (weight > 200);

if ( tall && heavy) printf("You could join the police force.\n");
if (!tall && !heavy) printf("Have you considered being a jockey?\n");
    ⋮
```

Program 3.7 further illustrates the use of logical variables. It must be pointed out that this is a rather clumsy program, which contains a lot of repetition in the if statement conditions. In Chapter 6 (Section 6.3) we shall be looking at how we can further develop our if-else structure, and a more efficient and more elegant version of this program will be presented.

━━━━━━━ **PROGRAM 3.7** ━━━━━━━

An insurance broker wishes to implement the following guidance table in a program, so that when an age, engine capacity and number of convictions are typed in, the appropriate message is displayed.

Age	Engine size	Convictions	Message
>=21	>=2000	>=3	policy loaded by 45%
>=21	>=2000	< 3	policy loaded by 15%
>=21	< 2000	>=3	policy loaded by 30%
>=21	< 2000	< 3	no loading
< 21	>=2000	>=3	no policy to be issued
< 21	>=2000	< 3	policy loaded by 60%
< 21	< 2000	>=3	policy loaded by 50%
< 21	< 2000	< 3	policy loaded by 10%

```c
/* Program 3.7 : Insurance Policy */
#include <stdio.h>
void main(void)
{
  int age, cc, convictions;
  int over21, LargeCar, RiskDriver;

  printf("Age?"); scanf("%i", &age);
  printf("cc?"); scanf("%i", &cc);
  printf("How many convictions?"); scanf("%i", &convictions);

  over21 = (age >= 21);
  LargeCar = (cc >= 2000);
  RiskDriver = (convictions >= 3);

  if (over21 && LargeCar && RiskDriver)
    printf("Policy loaded by 45 per cent.\n");

  if (over21 && LargeCar && !RiskDriver)
    printf("Policy loaded by 15 per cent.\n");

  if (over21 && !LargeCar && RiskDriver)
    printf("Policy loaded by 30 per cent.\n");

  if (over21 && !LargeCar && !RiskDriver)
    printf("No loading.\n");

  if (!over21 && LargeCar && RiskDriver)
    printf("No policy to be issued.\n");

  if (!over21 && LargeCar && !RiskDriver)
    printf("Policy loaded by 60 per cent.\n");

  if (!over21 && !LargeCar && RiskDriver)
    printf("Policy loaded by 50 per cent.\n");

  if (!over21 && !LargeCar && !RiskDriver)
    printf("Policy loaded by 10 per cent.\n");

}
```

3.7 ■ Selecting one of many alternatives

There are many contexts in which we require a statement to select one out of a number of alternatives, as determined by a selector value. One way of doing this can be represented diagrammatically as shown in Figure 3.3.

We have replaced a condition that could have one of two values – TRUE or FALSE – with a more general selector. The two-valued condition which selected one out of two branches has been replaced by a quantity that can have more than two possible values and that can be used to select one out of a number of branches. Consider the following program fragment, which could be part of a program for controlling a coin-operated vending machine. Depending on the denomination or weight of the coin, one out of six totalizing instructions is selected and obeyed:

```
scanf("%i", &weight);
switch (weight)
{
   case 35 : credit += 50; break;
   case 19 : credit += 20; break;
   case 16 : credit += 10; break;
   case 9  : credit += 5;  break;
   case 7  : credit += 2;  break;
   case 3  : credit += 1;  break;
}
```

We are assuming that coins of denominations 50, 20, 10, 5, 2 and 1 have weights of 35, 19, 16, 9, 7 and 3, respectively. The structure is called a switch statement, and in this example the selector is (the value of) weight, which is an integer variable. weight should contain either 35, 19, 16, 9, 7 or 3. If it contains 9 then the fourth statement is selected. If it contains 3 then the last statement is selected. Thus one statement is selected – the statement whose label (after the keyword case) corresponds to the value of the selector. Notice that the keyword break occurs at the end of each line. If it is absent, execution continues through any subsequent cases until a break statement *is* encountered, or the end of the switch statement is reached.

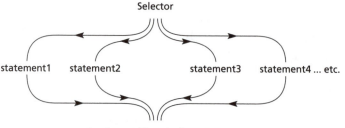

Figure 3.3 Selecting one out of many alternatives.

If the selector does not correspond with any of the cases, no statement is executed. However, there is a default option that can be added to take action for other values that might appear. Thus we could extend the above example as follows:

```
scanf("%i", &weight);
switch (weight)
{
   case 35 : credit += 50; break;
   case 19 : credit += 20; break;
   case 16 : credit += 10; break;
   case 9  : credit += 5;  break;
   case 7  : credit += 2;  break;
   case 3  : credit += 1;  break;
   default : printf("\nReject coin\n");
}
```

Any value of `weight` other than those listed will cause the default option to be obeyed.

More than one case can be associated with a statement, as follows:

```
scanf("%i", &month);
switch (month)
{
   case 1: case 2: case 11: case 12:
     printf("Low season rate.\n"); break;
   case 3: case 4: case 5: case 10:
     printf("Mid season rate.\n"); break;
   case 6: case 7: case 8: case 9:
     printf("Peak season rate.\n"); break;
}
```

The general form is:

switch (selector)
{
   one or more cases followed by one or more statements; break;
   one or more cases followed by one or more statements; break;
   one or more cases followed by one or more statements; break;

     ⋮

   optional default
}

The selector need not necessarily be a variable; it can be an arithmetic expression. Program 3.8 illustrates a context in which an expression would be employed. You should note that the expression must not yield a `float` result. In Program 3.8 the expression being used as a selector has type `int`.

In Program 3.8, note that the interest rate could not be conveniently calculated using a single expression because the variation of rate with loan size is not linear.

PROGRAM 3.8

The yearly rate of interest on a loan is:

```
   0 <  loan  < 1000      10%
1000 <= loan  < 2000      11%
2000 <= loan  < 3000      11.5%
3000 <= loan  < 4000      11.75%
4000 <= loan  < 5000      12%
5000 <= loan             13%
```

The program works out a year's interest given the size of the loan.

```c
/* Program 3.8 : Loan */

#include <stdio.h>

void main(void)
{
  int loan;
  float InterestRate;

  printf("Amount of loan?");  scanf("%i", &loan);

  switch (loan / 1000)
  {
    case 0:  InterestRate = 10;    break;
    case 1:  InterestRate = 11;    break;
    case 2:  InterestRate = 11.5;  break;
    case 3:  InterestRate = 11.75; break;
    case 4:  InterestRate = 12;    break;
    default: InterestRate = 13;
  }
  printf("Interest to pay: %.2f\n", loan * InterestRate/100);
}
```

If one of the actions to be selected in a `switch` statement involves obeying more than one C statement, then a sequence of statements can occur before the `break` statement, and they will all be executed. No braces are required.

━━━━━━━━ **SUMMARY OF CHAPTER 3** ━━━━━━━━

Key points

■ In this chapter we introduced our first **control statement**. The if statement has a **condition** and an action to perform if the condition is TRUE.

■ Conditions are created from expressions using the **relational operators**.

■ In an if-else statement, there is a second action, which will be carried out when the test condition is FALSE.

■ A compound statement can be made by enclosing a group of statements in braces.

■ More complex conditions can be created by using logical operators to combine subconditions.

■ The switch statement allows one of many options to be selected, depending on the value of an integer expression.

Good programming practice

■ **Indent** subsidiary blocks with additional space characters and line up the braces at the start and end of each block – this makes your code easier to read and debug.

■ In non-trivial expressions, use extra brackets to make your intentions clear.

Common problems	
Problem	**Symptom**
Using = instead of == in a condition, for example if(i=3) instead of if(i==3).	Your C system may give you a warning, but the program will still run, the condition will always be TRUE and any variable on the left of the = will be wrongly changed. Program behaviour will be unexpected.
Wrongly placed semicolons, for example after if(condition) or after else.	if statement behaviour will be unexpected.
Comparing floating point values with ==, instead of, for example, if(fabs(x-y)<0.001).	Condition will rarely be TRUE. Program behaviour will be unpredictable.
Missing braces round compound statement.	Only first statement will be covered by conditional. Program behaviour will be unexpected.

Problem *(continued)*	Symptom *(continued)*
Missing `break` in `case` branch.	More than one branch of the `case` statement will be obeyed. Program behaviour will be unexpected.
Missing space between word `case` and value, for example `case19:` instead of `case 19:`.	No error messages – the `case` label will be treated as an ordinary label (not used in this book). Program behaviour will be unexpected.
Value of `switch` expression does not match a `case` label.	The `case` statement will do nothing.

Debugging **tip**s

■ Place an extra `printf` in each branch of any suspect conditional statements. Note: this will require that each branch is made into a compound statement by adding braces if they are not already there.

■ In any suspect `switch` statements, include a default option that prints the value of the `switch` expression.

EXERCISES FOR CHAPTER 3

(1) Write an electricity bill program similar in specification to Program 1.7 but take into account the fact that a meter goes back to zero after reaching 9999, making the previous reading greater than the present.

(2) Write a program that calculates the discount, if any, on a sale. Sales of $100 and over are eligible for a 10% discount.

(3) Write a program to accept two items of information: a British shoe size and a 1 or 0 to indicate a man's or woman's shoe. The program is to output the American size according to the table:

```
Men's shoes:
British     7     8     9     10     11
American    7.5   8.5   9.5   10.5   11.5

Women's shoes:
British     3     4     5     6     7
American    4.5   5.5   6.5   7.5   8.5
```

(4) An educational establishment gives 10 courses numbered 1–10. Each course is given during two separate one-hour periods and some courses take place concurrently as follows:

Course	1,2	Thu	9 a.m.	Fri	10 a.m.
Course	3	Mon	10 a.m.	Thu	10 a.m.
Course	4,5	Mon	11 a.m.	Tue	11 a.m.
Course	6,7	Tue	9 a.m.	Wed	2 p.m.
Course	8	Mon	12 a.m.	Thu	9 a.m.
Course	9	Tue	10 a.m.	Wed	11 a.m.
Course	10	Fri	9 a.m.	Fri	11 a.m.

Write a timetable enquiry program that is to accept a course number and print a message giving the time periods at which the course is held.

(5) At the educational establishment of the previous exercise the days of the week are numbered 1–5 and the hours of each day are numbered 1–6. (Hour 1 is at 9 a.m. and Hour 6 is at 2 p.m.) A period is coded as a two-digit integer where the first digit gives the day and the second digit gives the hour of a period. Thus, for example, 23 means Tuesday at 11 a.m. Write a program that accepts as input a single integer period code and that outputs the numbers of any courses taking place during that period.

(6) Write a program that reads three integers representing an abbreviated date; for example:
    - Enter a 4 digit year

    26 12 94

and that will print the date in full; for example:

    26th December 1994

The day should be followed by an appropriate suffix, 'st', 'nd', 'rd' or 'th'.

(7) Write a program that will read the number of a month and, assuming that it is not a leap year, will print the number of days in the month.

(8) Extend your solution to Exercise 7 so that the program accepts the number of a month and the number of a year (which may be a leap year). It should print the number of days in the month.

(9) Return to Chapter 2, Exercise 5 and extend your program to calculate the number of extra tiles required for cutting. (Assume that the tiles are not symmetrical, and that a piece cut off a tile at one wall cannot be turned and used at another wall.)

CHAPTER 4

Simple counter-controlled loops

In this chapter we introduce a control statement that will allow us to make better use of the vast speed at which a computer can operate – a simple **loop** facility with which we can tell the computer to obey a section of program over and over again.

4.1 ■ Preliminary example

It is important at this stage to realize that a variable is just what the term *variable* says it is – its value can change while a program is being obeyed. Consider the behaviour of Program 4.1.

Let us assume that Program 4.1 is provided with input:

```
36 7 19
```

When the first `scanf` statement has been obeyed, we have the situation:

　　sum ⎡0⎤　　　next ⎡36⎤

When the assignment statement on the next line is obeyed, the expression on the right is evaluated first, regardless of what appears on the left. At this stage, `sum + next` has the value 36 and this value is placed in the variable `sum`, destroying or overwriting the value previously stored there:

　　sum ⎡36⎤　　　next ⎡36⎤

The next `scanf` statement causes the next number in the input to be stored in the variable `next`, again overwriting the value previously stored there. `sum + next` now has the value 43 and the next statement places this value in `sum`.

　　sum ⎡43⎤　　　next ⎡7⎤

After obeying the next two statements we have the situation

　　sum ⎡62⎤　　　next ⎡19⎤

======================================= PROGRAM 4.1 =======================================

This program adds three numbers together.

```
/* Program 4.1 : Add three numbers */

#include <stdio.h>

void main(void)
{
    int next, sum;
    sum = 0;

    scanf("%i", &next);
    sum = sum + next;

    scanf("%i", &next);
    sum = sum + next;

    scanf("%i", &next);
    sum = sum + next;

    printf("%i\n", sum);

}
```

Thus sum holds four different values while the program is being obeyed and next holds three. The net effect of the program is to add together the three numbers presented in the input. This is done by repeatedly obeying the two statements

```
scanf("%i", &next);
sum = sum + next;
```

4.2 ■ Simple for statements

We now present the first of the three looping statements available in C. These are all used to tell the computer to obey a group of one or more statements again and again. Instead of writing the above three statements in full three times, we can tell the computer to obey these statements three times by using a **for statement**, as in Program 4.2.

There are several points to note here:

■ The for statement tells the computer to obey the statements within the braces three times before carrying on to the next statement. The details of the notation that achieves this will be discussed shortly.

PROGRAM 4.2

This program is equivalent in effect to Program 4.1.

```
/* Program 4.2 : Add three numbers */

#include <stdio.h>

void main(void)
{
   int next, sum, count;
   sum = 0;
   for (count = 1; count <= 3; count++)
   {
      scanf("%i", &next);
      sum = sum + next;
   }
   printf("%i\n", sum);
}
```

- As in Chapter 3, braces {...} have been used to show that a group of statements belong together and are to be thought of as a single compound statement. Between these braces, we always have a list of statements (two in this case), each terminated by a semicolon. Thus, in this example, the complete sequence of statements between the inner { and } is obeyed three times before the printf statement is obeyed. Always use indentation (extra spaces) and line up the braces for a compound statement so that the body of the loop stands out from the surrounding program.
- count is an integer variable that is given the value 1 the first time the compound statement is obeyed, 2 the second time and 3 the third time. The computer uses this variable to count the number of times the compound statement has been obeyed. count is called the **control variable** of the for statement. Until we get to Chapter 8, the control variable will always be an integer variable and must be declared as such. As you will see shortly, there is no special significance in the name 'count' – we could have given the control variable any name we chose.
- Remember that a semicolon is used to terminate each complete statement. In Program 4.2, there is no semicolon at the end of the line of code containing the keyword for. This is because the for statement is not complete until the end of the statement block in braces. If a semicolon did occur before the opening brace, it would terminate the for statement prematurely, and the code would have a completely different meaning, which we shall look at shortly.

The behaviour of the for statement when obeyed can be illustrated diagrammatically as shown in Figure 4.1, hence the use of the term **loop**.

It is instructive to consider the effect of omitting the braces that enclose the compound statement:

```
sum = 0;
for (count = 1; count <= 3; count++)
   scanf("%i", &next);
   sum = sum + next;
```

Only the statement that immediately follows the control structure is obeyed repeatedly and in the absence of { and } this consists only of:

```
scanf("%i", &next);
```

Despite the indentation, the last line is not part of the loop and the above is equivalent in effect to:

```
sum = 0;
scanf("%i", &next);
scanf("%i", &next);
scanf("%i", &next);
sum = sum + next;
```

This reads a number into next, then reads another, overwriting the previous one, then reads a third. Only the third number is added to the variable sum.

And if the programmer accidentally typed a semicolon at the end of the first line of the for statement:

```
for (count=1; count <= 3; count++) ;
```

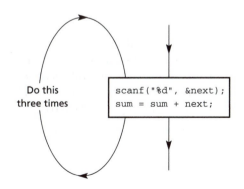

Figure 4.1 The behaviour of a simple for statement.

the computer would carry out the loop, doing *nothing* on each iteration because that unwanted semicolon is understood by the computer to be the terminator of an empty statement and that is all that will be repeated. The program would then go on to read only *one* number and add it to sum.

It is sensible to type the program in such a way that the meaning is made clear to the human reader. A few extra spaces are usually inserted before the lines containing statements that are to be obeyed repeatedly, thus making these statements stand out in the text. However, you should always remember that this use of layout does not affect the meaning of the program.

4.3 ■ Syntax of the `for` statement

In general, the `for` statement has the form:

for (initialization; condition; increment)
  statement;

or

for (initialization; condition; increment)
{
  statement1;
  statement2;
  etc. ...
}

The behaviour of our simple `for` statement is determined by the contents of the parentheses. Throughout this book, we shall assume that these always relate to a single control variable.

■ The **initialization** should be an assignment statement that gives the control variable a starting value. In our first simple example:

```
for (count = 1; count <= 3; count++)
```

the control variable count starts at 1.
■ The **condition** should be an expression that determines when the loop will end. In this case the loop is executed for values of count up to and including 3.
■ The **increment** tells the computer what to do with the control variable after each iteration. Here count is simply increased by one each time.

So, in general, if you want a loop to execute n times, your `for` statement should be:

```
for (i = 1; i <= n; i++) { ... }
```

or alternatively:

```
for (i = 0; i < n; i++) { ... }
```

In the second version, the loop will be iterated the same number of times, but the control variable starts from zero. If the control variable is not used in the body of the loop (see Section 4.5), these two versions have the same effect.

Our `for` statement which adds three numbers can be easily modified so as to add together ten numbers, say:

```
for (count = 1; count <= 10; count++)
{
    scanf("%i", &next);
    sum = sum + next;
}
```

We need not even commit ourselves to a fixed number of values to be added together. If the input supplied to the program starts with an integer telling the program how many numbers are to be added together, we could write

```
int next, sum, count, NumberOfValues;

scanf("%i", &NumberOfValues); sum = 0;

for (count = 1; count <= NumberOfValues; count++)
{
    scanf("%i", &next);
    sum = sum + next;
}
```

This program would then accept input such as:

```
5 26 72 41 32 61
```

and would add together the last five numbers. Input of:

```
2 15 42
```

would result in the addition of the two numbers 15 and 42. Note that input of 0 would result in execution of the loop zero times. No further data would be read and the final sum would be 0. This would be an odd thing to do in the present context, but at the heart of a large program there could be circumstances where the result of some calculation indicates that the body of a loop should not be executed at all.

4.4 ■ Loan repayment example

Now let us revisit the loan repayment example, introduced in Program 1.3. An alternative method for calculating and printing the outstanding balance after one repayment would be:

```
debt = debt + debt*MonthlyRate/100 - payment;
printf("Debt after next payment is %.2f\n", debt);
```

Here the assignment statement calculates the new balance owing and then stores it in the variable debt, destroying the previous contents of that variable. The advantage of expressing the calculation in this form is that it can now be obeyed repeatedly by using it in a for statement, as in Program 4.3.

PROGRAM 4.3

This program prints a month by month statement for a year's repayments on a loan.

```
/* Program 4.3 : Loan Repayment */

#include <stdio.h>

void main(void)
{
   float debt, MonthlyRate, payment;
   int month;

   printf("\nDebt:");  scanf("%f", &debt);
   printf("\nMonthly rate of interest:");  scanf("%f", &MonthlyRate);
   printf("\nMonthly payment:");  scanf("%f", &payment);

   for (month = 1; month <= 12; month++)
   {
     debt = debt + debt*MonthlyRate/100 - payment;
     printf("Debt after next payment is %.2f\n", debt);
   }
}
```

Given input:

```
Debt:95.00
Monthly rate of interest:2
Monthly payment:5
```

this program produces output:

```
Debt after next payment is 91.90
Debt after next payment is 88.74
Debt after next payment is 85.51
Debt after next payment is 82.22
Debt after next payment is 78.87
Debt after next payment is 75.44
Debt after next payment is 71.95
Debt after next payment is 68.39
Debt after next payment is 64.76
```

```
Debt after next payment is 61.06
Debt after next payment is 57.28
Debt after next payment is 53.42
```

Note that in writing this program we have assumed that the debt will not be paid off in the first year. If this does happen the computer will still do exactly what we have told it to do. Input of:

```
Debt: 272
Monthly rate of interest: 2.5
Monthly payment: 29
```

will result in output:

```
Debt after next payment is 249.80
Debt after next payment is 227.04
Debt after next payment is 203.72
Debt after next payment is 179.81
Debt after next payment is 155.31
Debt after next payment is 130.19
Debt after next payment is 104.45
Debt after next payment is 78.06
Debt after next payment is 51.01
Debt after next payment is 23.28
Debt after next payment is -5.13
Debt after next payment is -34.26
```

In Program 3.3, we detected whether overpayment had taken place after a single payment by using an appropriate if statement at the end of the program. We could make a similar test in Program 4.3, at the end of the year, by inserting a similar if statement after the for loop, just before the final brace of the program:

```
if (debt < 0)
   printf("Debt cleared. Refund = %.2f\n", -debt);
else
   printf("Debt after this year is %.2f\n", debt);
```

More appropriate methods of dealing with this will be discussed in Chapter 5.

4.5 ■ Making use of the control variable

As we have already remarked, the control variable is used by the computer to count how many times the statement (or compound statement) following the control structure has been obeyed. However, there is no reason why the programmer should not also make use of the value of this variable. As a simple example, the statement:

```
for (i = 1; i <= 10; i++) printf("%i ", i);
```

will print the integers from 1 to 10 all on one line. Program 4.4 extends Program 4.3 by printing the value of the control variable on each cycle of the loop.

═══════════════════ **PROGRAM 4.4** ═══════════════════

This is similar to Program 4.3, except that each month number is tabulated alongside the outstanding debt.

```
/* Program 4.4 : Loan Statement */

#include <stdio.h>

void main(void)
{
   float debt, MonthlyRate, payment;
   int month;

   printf("\nDebt:");  scanf("%f", &debt);
   printf("\nMonthly rate of interest:");  scanf("%f", &MonthlyRate);
   printf("\nMonthly payment:");  scanf("%f", &payment);

   printf("\nmonth   outstanding debt\n");

   for (month = 1; month <= 12; month++)
   {
      debt = debt + debt*MonthlyRate/100 - payment;
      printf("%5i%19.2f\n", month, debt);
   }

}
```

Given input:

```
Debt:1256.75
Monthly rate of interest:1.25
Monthly payment:56.50
```

this program will print:

```
month      outstanding debt
    1            1215.96
    2            1174.66
    3            1132.84
    4            1090.50
    5            1047.63
```

6	1004.23
7	960.28
8	915.79
9	870.73
10	825.12
11	778.93
12	732.17

The first time the statement:

```
printf("%5i%19.2f\n", month, debt);
```

is obeyed month has the value 1, the second time it has the value 2 and so on. The formatting information in this statement has been chosen so that each time the statement is obeyed, the two values printed are lined up below the two headings which were output by the statement:

```
printf("month  outstanding debt\n")
```

A program can use a control variable in any way we like while the corresponding loop is being obeyed, except that the program should not attempt to change the control variable. This would be unreasonable because it would interfere, perhaps disastrously, with the only record there is of how many times the loop statement has been obeyed. In particular, this means that inside the loop the control variable should not appear on the left of any assignment statement or as a parameter of a scanf statement.

C is rather *laissez-faire* about such things and if you do change the control variable within the loop, your program will still be executed, possibly with unpredictable results. You should resist the temptation to do 'clever' things by tampering with the control variable within the loop and try to stick to using the for statement for simple counting loops of the type we have described. Other types of loops are better implemented using the statements described in Chapter 5.

4.6 ■ Other features of the for statement

Some further points about for statements are illustrated by the following examples:

```
for (number = -8; number <= 5; number++) printf("%i ", number);
```

When obeyed, this statement will output:

```
. -8 -7 -6 -5 -4 -3 -2 -1 0 1 2 3 4 5
```

In fact, the control variable need not simply be incremented in steps of 1. In order to print all of the even numbers from 2 to 100 we can use:

```
for (n = 2; n <= 100; n += 2) printf("%i ", n);
```

The odd numbers from 1 to 99 could be output by:

```
for (n = 1; n <= 99; n += 2) printf("%i ", n);
```

or, using a control variable ascending in steps of 1:

```
for (n = 1; n <= 50; n++) printf("%i ", 2*n - 1);
```

We can use any expression we like to specify the starting and finishing values for the control variable. For example, given two integers m and n (both greater than 1), we can print all of the integers from m+n to m*n by:

```
for (next = m+n; next <= m*n; next++) printf("%i ", next);
```

Finally, the control variable can be made to take values that decrease. For example, we can print the integers from 0 to 100 in reverse order by:

```
for (k = 100; k >= 0; k--) printf("%i ", k);
```

4.7 ■ Programs with more than one simple loop

Program 4.5 contains two `for` statements, written one after the other. When the program is obeyed, the first loop will be executed the appropriate number of times before the second is considered. The same control variable is used for both loops, but since only one loop is obeyed at a time, this does not lead to any conflict.

Output from this program will consist of:

```
Sale    Commission

   1          0.12
   2          0.25
   3          0.37
   4          0.50
   5          0.62
   :            :
  99         12.38
 100         12.50
 101         15.65
 102         15.81
   :            :
 199         30.84
 200         31.00
```

The reasons for using named constants in a program like this were discussed in Section 1.6.

PROGRAM 4.5

A salesperson receives commission on sales at a rate of 12.5% on sales worth $100 or less, and 15.5% on sales worth more than $100. This program prints a table that gives the value of the commission on any sale up to $200.

```c
/* Program 4.5 : Commission Table */

#include <stdio.h>
#define LOWER_RATE 0.125
#define HIGHER_RATE 0.155
#define TOP_OF_LOWER_RANGE 100

void main(void)
{
    int sale;
    printf("Sale  Commission\n\n");

    for (sale = 1; sale <= TOP_OF_LOWER_RANGE; sale++)
        printf("%4i%13.2f\n", sale, sale*LOWER_RATE);

    for (sale = TOP_OF_LOWER_RANGE+1; sale <= 200; sale++)
        printf("%4i%13.2f\n", sale, sale*HIGHER_RATE);

}
```

SUMMARY OF CHAPTER 4

Key points

■ A simple `for` loop with an integer **control variable** allows a block of code to be obeyed several times.

■ It is possible to defer making a decision about the number of iterations until run-time – this is done by making the upper bound for the control variable a value that is provided by the user.

■ It is possible (and sometimes useful) to refer to the control variable within the body of the loop.

Good programming practice

■ Use `for` loops only for counter-controlled loops. More appropriate techniques for implementing other types of loop are introduced in the next chapter.

■ Do not change the control variable within a loop.

Common problems	
Problem	**Symptom**
Wrongly placed semicolon after `for (...)`.	Loop will simply count up, doing nothing else, and the program will then obey the loop body once.
Missing braces around compound statement.	Only the first statement after the `for` heading will be repeated. The rest will then be obeyed only once.
`<` instead of `<=` in loop condition.	Loop will make one too few executions.
`<=` instead of `<` in loop condition.	Loop will make one too many executions.
Infinite loop. A crude example might be: `for (i = 1; i >= 0; i++) ...` This can happen more subtly if the start and stop values are stored in variables.	Loop will execute for ever. If there are `printf` or `scanf` statements in the loop, you should be able to interrupt it with a break (control-C or control-break on a PC), otherwise you may have to restart your machine.

Debugging tip

- At the start of any suspect loop, place an extra `printf` to print the control variable and any other values that may be helpful. This will not only provide a trace of what is happening, but will also enable you to break into the loop if it goes infinite.

EXERCISES FOR CHAPTER 4

scanf ("%G

(1) Write a program that reads and adds 15 floating point numbers and then prints their average. and the total

(2) Write a program that reads and multiplies together 20 floating point numbers.

(3) Write a program to print a 'four times table' in the form:

```
1 x 4 = 4
2 x 4 = 8
3 x 4 = 12
etc.
```

(4) Write a program that reads an integer, *n* say, and prints an '*n* times table'.

(5) Write a program that prints all multiples of 3 from 3 to 90.

(6) '*n* factorial' is defined as *n**(*n*-1)*(*n*-2)*. . .*3*2*1. Write a program that reads a value for *n* and calculates *n* factorial. When testing your program, you should bear in mind the remarks in Section 1.3 about the limits on the sizes of numbers that can be handled.

(7) Write a program that reads an integer *n* followed by *n* floating point numbers. The program should calculate and print the average of the numbers.

(8) An electricity board has previous and present meter readings for a known number of customers. Write a program that will read the appropriate number of pairs of readings and print a bill for each customer.

(9) Write a program that accepts the 20 examination marks obtained by a candidate and prints a 'pass/fail' message depending on whether the average is greater than or equal to 50, or less than 50.

(10) Twenty candidates have each taken two examination papers, paper 1 and paper 2. The marks obtained are to be typed as input for a computer program. The first two numbers typed are the marks obtained by the first candidate, the next two numbers are the marks obtained by the second candidate, and so on. Write a program that calculates and prints the overall average mark for paper 1, and the overall average mark for paper 2.

(11) A bank makes a service charge on a customer's account if the average daily balance over a 30-day period is less than £50. The charge, if applied, is 20p for each debit entry. Write a program that reads 30 pairs of values, where each pair consists of a daily balance and a count of the debit entries for the day. The program should print a message indicating whether there should be a service charge, and if so, how much.

(12) Write a program that reads the number of a year followed by the number of a month. It should then read a Celsius temperature for each day in the month and convert that temperature to Fahrenheit.

➡ **Hint**: Exercise 7 in Chapter 3 involved writing a program to calculate how many days there are in a given month. The program can be extended to use the value calculated to control the number of executions of a `for` loop.

Conditional loops

We saw in Chapter 4 how the computer can be told to obey a section of program a specified number of times. We frequently require the computer to obey a section of program repeatedly as long as some condition holds. As a practical analogy, we might instruct a person to keep putting items in a container while some space still remains. Such a construction is an example of a conditional loop, and C provides two conditional looping statements, which we introduce in this chapter.

5.1 ■ Simple `while` loops

Let us return to the loan repayment example discussed in Chapter 4. Suppose we want a program to print a month-by-month statement for the duration of the loan. As before, the computer must repeatedly obey the two statements:

```
debt += debt*MonthlyRate/100 - payment;
printf("Debt after next payment is %.2f\n", debt);
```

but only for as long as the outstanding debt is greater than the repayment that is about to be made. Program 5.1 implements this variation.

When a `while` loop is obeyed, the computer starts by testing the condition after the word `while`. If the outcome is TRUE, the statement (or statement block) after the condition is obeyed and the condition is tested again. The process is repeated as long the outcome of the test is TRUE. As soon as the outcome of the test is FALSE, the computer goes on and obeys the next statement.

This process can be illustrated diagrammatically as shown in Figure 5.1. Note that the condition used to control the `while` loop is evaluated before the loop is obeyed for the first time, and the loop may therefore not be obeyed at all. In fact the `while` loop is rather similar in structure (and in its initial behaviour) to an `if` statement.

Indentation has again been used in Program 5.1 to highlight the loop structure. You should be getting into the habit of doing this when typing your own programs.

PROGRAM 5.1

This program prints a month-by-month statement for the duration of the loan.

```
/* Program 5.1 : Complete Statement */
#include <stdio.h>
void main(void)
{
   float debt, MonthlyRate, payment;
   printf("\nDebt:");  scanf("%f", &debt);
   printf("\nMonthly rate of interest:");  scanf("%f", &MonthlyRate);
   printf("\nMonthly payment:");  scanf("%f", &payment);

   while (debt + debt*MonthlyRate/100 >= payment)
   {
      debt += debt*MonthlyRate/100 - payment;
      printf("Debt after next payment is %.2f\n", debt);
   }
   printf("\nFinal payment required will be %.2f\n",
                      debt + debt*MonthlyRate/100);
}
```

As was the case for the `for` statement, the erroneous use of a semicolon just after the `while` condition will terminate the `while` loop prematurely, but in this case the consequences can be even more disastrous. For example, if the `while` loop in Program 5.1 was mistyped as:

```
while (debt + debt*MonthlyRate/100 >= payment);
{
   debt += debt*MonthlyRate/100 - payment;
   printf("Debt after next payment is %.2f\n", debt);
}
```

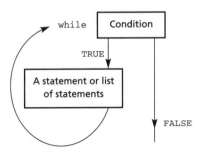

Figure 5.1 The behaviour of a simple `while` loop.

the empty statement introduced by the semicolon is all that will be repeated before the condition is evaluated again. Because nothing has changed, the condition will still be true and the loop will continue indefinitely, doing nothing on each cycle apart from repeatedly testing the same condition. On many systems, the only way to interrupt this loop will be to close down the C environment if there is a mechanism for doing this, or even to switch off and restart the whole machine.

In Program 5.1, the expression `debt + debt*MonthlyRate/100` was evaluated twice for each execution of the loop. We shall see how to avoid this in Section 5.6.

5.2 ■ Simple do **loops**

The second form of conditional loop provided in C is the do loop, which is illustrated in Program 5.2.

PROGRAM 5.2

A sequence of experimental readings have been taken at daily intervals and these readings (floating point numbers) are to be typed as input to this program. The readings are added together, one by one, and as soon as the total exceeds a specified threshold a message is printed indicating how many readings have been processed.

```c
/* Program 5.2 : Count Days */
#include <stdio.h>
#define THRESHOLD 100.0
void main(void)
{
  float NextReading, total;
  int days;
  days = 0; total = 0;
  do
  {
    days++;
    scanf("%f", &NextReading);
    total += NextReading;
  }
  while (total <= THRESHOLD);
  printf("Threshold total of %f has been exceeded.\n", THRESHOLD);
  printf("This occurred after %i days.\n", days);
}
```

When a do loop is obeyed, the computer starts by obeying the statement (or statement block) between the words do and while. The condition after the word while is then tested. Provided the outcome of the test is TRUE, the statements between do and while are obeyed again and the condition tested once more. As long as the outcome of the test is TRUE, the process is repeated. When the outcome of the test is discovered to be FALSE, the computer goes on to obey the next statement. This process can be illustrated diagrammatically as shown in Figure 5.2.

Program 5.3 uses a do loop to read data (a train timetable) until an entry is found that meets a required condition. Of course, nobody in their right mind would consider typing the train timetable each time they wanted to catch a train. By the time the data has been typed they will have missed the next train. We shall show how to avoid doing this in the next section.

If the earliest possible time specified is 1200 and the timetable contains the following information:

```
0806     0906
0901     0955
1155     1259
1215     1316
1450     1555
1645     1750
```

the output produced will be:

```
Your train leaves at 1215 and arrives at 1316
```

Note that the loop is obeyed only four times before the terminating condition is satisfied. Since the scanf statement is contained within the loop, only the first four lines of the timetable will be required as input by the program.

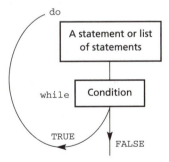

Figure 5.2 The behaviour of a simple do loop.

PROGRAM 5.3

A businessperson wants a program that will read a train timetable and that will find the first train to leave after a specified time. The input for the program consists of the earliest possible departure time, followed by a list of the departure and arrival times of suitable trains. The train times are in chronological order and are expressed in the 24-hour clock system. The program finds the first train that leaves after the earliest time specified and reports its departure and arrival times.

```
/* Program 5.3 : Next Train */

#include <stdio.h>

void main(void)
{
   int earliest, depart, arrive;

   printf("Earliest possible depart time?");  scanf("%i", &earliest);

   printf("Now input the timetable:\n");

   do
      scanf("%i%i", &depart, &arrive);
   while (depart < earliest);

   printf("Your train leaves at %i ", depart);
   printf("and arrives at %i\n", arrive);
}
```

5.3 ■ Reading data from text files

Program 5.3 will be very tedious to use, and rather pointless, if someone has to sit and type the timetable each time the program is obeyed. Instead, the timetable could be typed once into a file on disk so that subsequently a program can read the information back from the file. The data does not then have to be typed afresh every time the program is tested or used. The way you type text into a file will depend on the computer system you are using, but the process will be similar to the way you have been typing your C programs and saving them. In fact you will probably be able to use the same editor that you have been using for preparing your C programs. When you save some text that is to be used as a data file by programs, you should use a name for the file that makes this clear. For example, on a PC, you could use file names that end with the extension .DAT instead of the extension .C that has probably been used so far for your C program files.

Program 5.4 illustrates the changes needed for Program 5.3 to read its data from a previously typed timetable file.

PROGRAM 5.4

This is the same as Program 5.3, but the timetable data is read from a previously typed file called TIMES.DAT.

```
/* Program 5.4 : Next Train 2 */

#include <stdio.h>

void main(void)
{
    int earliest, depart, arrive;
    FILE *timetable;

    printf("Earliest possible depart time?");  scanf("%i", &earliest);

    timetable = fopen("TIMES.DAT", "r");

    do
        fscanf(timetable, "%i%i", &depart, &arrive);
    while (depart < earliest);

    printf("Your train leaves at %i ", depart);
    printf("and arrives at %i\n", arrive);

    fclose(timetable);

}
```

There are a number of points to note about handling input from a text file:

■ A **file variable** is used by the program to keep track of the status of the file as the data in it is being read. This is defined in Program 5.4 by:

```
FILE *timetable;
```

■ The file must be opened before reading from it:

```
timetable = fopen("TIMES.DAT", "r");
```

TIMES.DAT is the name given to the file when it was created using your editor. The code "r" means the file is for reading ("w" is used to indicate that a program is going to write to a file). In the absence of other information, this file must be in the same file directory that is used to run the program.

■ To read from the file, we use `fscanf` instead of `scanf`, and include the name of the file variable at the start of the list inside the parentheses.

```
fscanf(timetable, "%i%i", &depart, &arrive);
```

■ The file is closed after the program has finished reading data.

```
fclose(timetable);
```

This version of the timetable program will cause problems if the user requests a departure time later than the last train. The program will keep trying to read data beyond the end of the file. The onus is on the programmer to incorporate tests that recognize this possibility and stop it from happening. A special function, called `feof`, is available. This can be used to recognize that we have attempted to read beyond the end of a file. We shall illustrate ways of using this function in Sections 5.7 and 5.8.

5.4 ■ `while` **loops versus** `do` **loops**

The main difference between these two constructions is that in a `while` loop the condition is evaluated at the start of the loop and the body of the loop may not be executed at all, whereas with a `do` loop, the body of the loop is always executed at least once before the condition is encountered. Any conditional loop can be implemented using a `while` loop, provided that care is taken to ensure that the condition at the start can be legally evaluated before the body of the loop has been executed for the first time. The same is not true of a `do` loop.

Some authorities would advocate the exclusive use of the `while` loop for the implementation of conditional loops on the grounds that any conditional looping situation can be covered by using one language construction instead of arbitrarily choosing between two very similar ones. While sympathizing with this view, we shall continue to make occasional use of `do` loops.

In some examples, the choice of which type of loop to use is largely a matter of personal taste. For example, the loop in Program 5.2 could have been equally well expressed as:

```
while (total <= THRESHOLD)
{
    days++;
    scanf("%f", &NextReading);
    total += NextReading;
}
```

In some examples where we could use either statement, the use of a `while` loop is a little clumsy. For example, in order to express the loop of Program 5.4 using a `while` loop, we need to insert an extra `fscanf` statement in order that the `while` condition can be evaluated before the loop has been obeyed for the first time:

```
fscanf(timetable, "%i%i", &depart, &arrive);
while (depart < earliest);
   fscanf(timetable, "%i%i", &depart, &arrive);
```

Finally, there are some examples in which only the `while` loop is satisfactory. Program 5.5 illustrates such a situation.

PROGRAM 5.5

This program types out a simple sum for the person sitting at the keyboard to attempt. The program then reads the answer which is typed. As long as the answer is wrong, the person sitting at the keyboard is asked to try again. An appropriate message is output when the correct answer has eventually been typed.

```
/* Program 5.5 : Arithmetic Test */

#include <stdio.h>
#define A 16
#define B 25

void main(void)
{
   int attempts, answer;
   printf("Let's test your arithmetic.\n");
   printf("Type the answer to the following sum.\n");
   printf("%i + %i = ", A, B);
   scanf("%i", &answer); attempts = 1;
   while (answer != A+B)
   {
      printf("\nWrong - try again.\n");
      printf("%i + %i = ", A, B);
      scanf("%i", &answer); attempts++;
   }
   printf("\n");
   if (attempts == 1)
      printf("Very good - you got it in one!\n");
   else printf("You got it at last!\n");

   printf("Bye for now!\n");
}
```

When executed, this program might produce a display such as:

```
Let's test your arithmetic.
Type the answer to the following sum.
16 + 25 = 42

Wrong - try again.
16 + 25 = 41

You got it at last!
Bye for now!
```

The numbers 42 and 41 have been typed by the user, and the rest by the program. If the user types the correct answer the first time, it would clearly be unsatisfactory for the statements in the loop to be obeyed at all. This is a trivial example of a Computer Assisted Learning (CAL) program. A more realistic program would generate random numbers for A and B and would then use these numbers.

It will be interesting to look at the changes needed to Program 5.5 in order for it to generate random numbers for the arithmetic test. We can do this by using the standard functions randomize and random from stdlib.h as follows:

```
#include <stdio.h>
#include <stdlib.h>
#include <time.h>

void main(void)
{
    int attempts, answer;
    int A,B;
    randomize();
    A=random(28)+2;
    B=random(28)+2;
              ⋮
```

The changes shown will ensure that a different pair of values is presented to the user each time the program is run. The expression random(28) will have a random value in the range 0–27, so that random(28)+2 will be a value in the range 2–29 (using the values 0 or 1 in the arithmetic test would make it too easy!).

The call to randomize is necessary because of the way the random function works. Each time random is called, it remembers the previous value that was generated and does some arithmetic on it to generate the next number. This arithmetic has been carefully developed by statisticians to make sure that any sequence of numbers produced will be uniformly distributed. (So they are not really random numbers at all!) In the absence of randomize, random would start in the same place each time the program was run and would thus generate the same question each time. The call to randomize ensures that the random number generator starts in a different place each time the program is used. The starting point is calculated from the current time on the system clock, hence the need to include the library `time.h` in the program heading.

When developing a program that uses random numbers, it can often be a good idea to leave out the call to `randomize` during the testing and debugging stages. This will mean that the program will use the same numbers each time it is run, thus making it much easier to track down any problems. Once the program has been thoroughly tested in this way, a call to `randomize` can then be inserted at the start.

5.5 ∎ Multiple terminating conditions

In Programs 4.3 and 4.4 we printed a month-by-month statement for the first 12 monthly repayments of a loan. As we mentioned, these programs will produce nonsensical results if the loan is paid off in less than a year. Program 5.1 ensures that the debt does not become negative, but insists on printing a statement for the duration of the loan, however long that may be. Program 5.6 combines the two different stopping conditions.

PROGRAM 5.6

This prints a month-by-month statement for the first 12 monthly repayments of a loan, or for the duration of the loan if that is less than 12 months.

```
/* Program 5.6 : Loan Statement */

#include <stdio.h>

void main(void)
{
   float debt, MonthlyRate, payment;
   int month;

   printf("\nDebt:");   scanf("%f", &debt);
   printf("\nMonthly rate of interest:");   scanf("%f", &MonthlyRate);
   printf("\nMonthly payment:");   scanf("%f", &payment);

   printf("\nMonth   Outstanding debt\n\n");

   month = 0;

   while ( (month < 12) &&
           (debt + debt*MonthlyRate/100 >= payment) )
   {
      month++;
      debt += debt*MonthlyRate/100 - payment;
      printf("%5i%19.2f\n", month, debt);
   }
```

```
    printf("\n");
    if (month < 12)
    {
       printf("Debt cleared within a year.\n");
       printf("Final payment: ");
       printf("%.2f\n", debt + debt*MonthlyRate/100);
    }
}
```

You should avoid the temptation to use the C for loop to combine a counting loop with additional conditions. C allows you to do this by putting more complex conditions in the heading of the for loop, but doing this obscures the exact structure of the loop being specified. for loops should be used only for implementing simple counting loops, and while loops should be used where more elaborate conditions are involved.

As another example, consider the problem of a meteorologist who requires programs that can be used to analyse the weather readings for a particular year. In Program 5.7, there are two reasons why the program might stop obeying the loop. In order to test why the loop terminated and print an appropriate message, the program has to re-test the main stopping condition with an if statement. Note that it would have been wrong for the if statement to use the condition day != 365 instead, as this would not result in an appropriate message in the case where the last day of the year was found to satisfy the temperature and sunshine requirements. Neater ways of dealing with this will be discussed later.

PROGRAM 5.7

This program reads, from a file, input that consists of 365 pairs of values, one pair for each day of the year. The first number in each pair is the average temperature for the day and the second is the number of hours of sunshine for the day. The program counts how many days elapsed before the first day on which both the average temperature exceeded 15 degrees and the number of hours of sunshine exceeded 10. The program caters for the possibility that there is no such day.

```
/* Program 5.7 : Heat Wave */

#include <stdio.h>
#define TEMP_THRESHOLD 15.0
#define SUN_THRESHOLD 10.0

void main(void)
{
```

```
float NextTemp, NextSun;
int day;
FILE *WeatherFile;

day = 0;
WeatherFile = fopen("WEATHER.DAT", "r");
do
{
  day++;
  fscanf(WeatherFile, "%f%f", &NextTemp, &NextSun);
} while ( ((NextTemp <= TEMP_THRESHOLD) ||
          (NextSun  <= SUN_THRESHOLD)
        ) && (day != 365) );

if ( (NextTemp > TEMP_THRESHOLD)
  && (NextSun > SUN_THRESHOLD) )
  {
    printf("There were %i ", day-1);
    printf("days before the first good day.\n");
  }
else
  printf("That was an exceptionally bad year.\n");

fclose(WeatherFile);
}
```

5.6 ■ Data terminators

We saw in Chapter 4 how we could instruct the computer to read and process a given number of values supplied as input. In Program 4.2, the number of items to be handled was fixed at three. Each time this program is obeyed, three values have to be supplied as input. In Chapter 4, we also demonstrated how the number of values to be handled could be indicated by a number typed at the start of a program's input. Each time such a program is obeyed, a different number of values can be processed and the person supplying the input will have to know how many values there are before data input can start. This is not always convenient, particularly where the number of values to be processed is large.

Here we present a widely used alternative approach. The input starts with the sequence of values to be processed and a special value is typed at the end of the input to indicate that there are no further values. Such a special value is called a **data terminator**.

━━━━━━━━━━━━━━━━━━━━ **PROGRAM 5.8** ━━━━━━━━━━━━━━━━━━━━

This program reads and adds a sequence of positive floating point numbers (at least one). In this program the data terminator is any negative number.

```c
/* Program 5.8 : Add */

#include <stdio.h>

void main(void)
{
  float sum, next;
  sum = 0.0;
  scanf("%f", &next);
  while (next >= 0)
  {
    sum += next;
    scanf("%f", &next);
  }

  printf("Sum is %f\n", sum);
}
```

Program 5.8 illustrates a common feature of conditional loops: the next value to be processed is obtained at the end of the loop so that this value is tested before it is processed. This necessitates obtaining the first value before entering the loop.

A similar structure is required in Programs 5.1 and 5.6 if we wish to avoid evaluating the expression:

```c
debt + debt*MonthlyRate/100
```

twice during each execution of the loop. We can use something like:

```c
scanf("%f%f%f", &debt, &MonthlyRate, &payment);

debt += debt*MonthlyRate/100;
while (debt >= payment)
{
  debt -= payment;
  printf("Debt after next payment is %.2f\n", debt);
  debt += debt*MonthlyRate/100;
}

printf("\nFinal payment required will be ");
printf("%.2f\n", debt);
```

Here we add a month's interest to debt at the end of the loop so that this new value of debt can be tested before the next payment is subtracted at the beginning of the loop. In some ways, this is a much cleaner solution, as the value of the variable debt always represents exactly the amount outstanding on the loan at every stage during the execution of the program.

Using a do loop would not eliminate the necessity of obtaining the first value before entering the loop or of obtaining the next value at the end of the loop. The best version of Program 5.8 using a do loop is:

```
sum = 0.0;
scanf ("%f", &next);
do
{ sum += next;
    scanf ("%f", &next);
} while (next >= 0)
```

The only disadvantage of this version is that the input list must contain at least one number before the data terminator. This is not important in the present context as we are unlikely to request the program to add up a list of zero numbers. However, in the heart of a large program, where we are processing a list of items that satisfy some complex condition, it is quite common for there to be no items that meet the required condition; hence, the while loop is the safer alternative.

It is interesting to consider a number of alternative constructions for the loop in Program 5.8, all of which are occasionally produced by beginners and all of which are *wrong*. (Similar erroneous versions can be constructed using while loops.) The first version would add the data terminator, which is a negative number, to the total:

```
sum = 0.0;
do {
    scanf ("%f", &next);
    sum += next;
}   while (next >= 0);
```

The next version would not add the first number to the total and would again add the data terminator to the total:

```
sum = 0.0;
scanf ("%f", &next);
do {
    scanf ("%f",   &next);
    sum +=  next;
}   while   (next >= 0);
```

The next version adds together the first, third, fifth, etc. numbers in the data and tests the second, fourth, sixth, etc:

```
sum = 0.0;
do  {
    scanf  ("%f",   &next);
    sum +=  next;
    scanf  ("%f",   &next);
}   while  (next >= 0);
```

If the numbers in the input are being handled in groups of two or more, care has to be taken in handling data terminators. The neatest solution is to insert a group of data terminators that contains the same number of values as the groups into which the rest of the data is organized. This is illustrated in Program 5.9.

PROGRAM 5.9

Voting takes place for two political parties in a number of constituencies. The two vote-totals for each constituency are typed in pairs as input to a program and two negative numbers are typed in the input when all pairs of totals have been typed. This program adds up the overall totals for the two parties and reports the overall result.

```
/* Program 5.9 : Election */
#include <stdio.h>
void main(void)
{
    int Party1Next, Party2Next,
        Party1Overall, Party2Overall;

    Party1Overall = 0; Party2Overall = 0;
    scanf ("%i%i", &Party1Next, &Party2Next);
    while (Party1Next >= 0)
    {
        Party1Overall += Party1Next;
        Party2Overall += Party2Next;
        scanf ("%i%i", &Party1Next, &Party2Next);
    }
    printf ("Party 1: %i\n", Party1Overall);
    printf ("Party 2: %i\n", Party2Overall);
}
```

If presented with input:

```
3   7
5   9
4   2
-1  -1
```

Program 5.9 will output:

```
party1: 12
party2: 18
```

The logical structure of this program is the same as that of Program 5.8, except that the input values are processed in pairs. Two data terminators are needed in order that they can be read by the same statement that reads the other pairs of values. (The test for termination of the loop needs to examine only the first value of each pair.) If we wish to type only one negative value at the end of the input data, a slightly more difficult structure is required for the loop:

```
scanf("%i", &Party1Next);
while (Party1Next >= 0
{
   scanf("%i", &Party2Next);
   Party1Overall += Party1Next;
   Party2Overall += Party2Next;
   scanf("%i", &Party1Next);
}
```

This version reads only one number at the end of the loop and tests it. Only if this value is not the terminator can a second value be safely read.

Finally, Program 5.10 illustrates the use of two while loops one after the other. Each loop deals with a separate set of data with its own data terminator.

As was the case in Program 4.5, the second loop is not encountered until the first loop has been obeyed the appropriate number of times. The first while loop is obeyed until the first negative number is read and only then can the program carry on to obey the next loop. The input for the program will take the form:

```
3   5   4   -1
7   9   2   -1
```

or even:

```
2   3   7   9   4   -1
1   7   6   -1
```

if candidates for party 1 are standing for election in more constituencies than are candidates for party 2.

━━━━━━━━━━━━━━━━━ **PROGRAM 5.10** ━━━━━━━━━━━━━━━━━

This program adds up the overall totals for the two parties in an election, but the constituency subtotals for one party are all typed first in the input and are terminated by a negative number. The subtotals for the second party are then typed and are also terminated by a negative number.

```c
/* Program 5.10 : Election 2 */

#include <stdio.h>

void main(void)
{
  int Party1Next, Party2Next,
      Party1Overall, Party2Overall;

  Party1Overall = 0;
  scanf("%i", &Party1Next);
  while (Party1Next >= 0)
  {
    Party1Overall += Party1Next;
    scanf("%i", &Party1Next);
  }
  Party2Overall = 0;
  scanf("%i", &Party2Next);
  while (Party2Next >= 0)
  {
    Party2Overall += Party2Next;
    scanf("%i", &Party2Next);
  }
  printf("Party 1: %i\n", Party1Overall);
  printf("Party 2: %i\n", Party2Overall);
}
```

5.7 ■ Detecting the end of a data file

Program 5.8 could be rewritten to take data from a file instead of from the keyboard. If we include a negative number at the end of the data in the file, all we need to do is to use fscanf instead of scanf:

```c
FILE *numbers;
numbers = fopen("NUMBERS.DAT","r");
```

```
sum = 0.0;
fscanf(numbers, "%f", &next);
while (next >= 0)
{
    sum += next;
    fscanf(numbers,"%f", &next);
}

    fclose(numbers);
```

However, we can detect the end of the file by using the feof function that was mentioned at the end of Section 5.3. This eliminates the need to include the negative data terminator in the file. To do this we use exactly the same program structure:

```
FILE *numbers;
numbers = fopen("NUMBERS.DAT","r");

sum = 0.0;
fscanf(numbers, "%f", &next);
while (! feof(numbers))
{
    sum += next;
    fscanf(numbers,"%f", &next);
}

fclose(numbers);
```

At each cycle of the loop, we attempt to obtain the next value and test that a valid data item has been read before going ahead and processing it. In this case, we detect whether the end of the data has been reached by using the feof function as illustrated. feof returns TRUE if the fscanf hit the end of the file while attempting to read a number. Thus the loop will not terminate until all of the numbers in the file have been read and processed.

5.8 ■ Use of logical variables

An integer used as a logical variable (see Section 3.6) often provides a neat way for a programmer to express the terminating condition for a loop, and to test subsequently why the loop was terminated. As an example, we shall rewrite Program 5.7 to use a variable in this way, giving Program 5.11.

As another example of this approach, we revisit Program 5.4 and examine a way of recognizing that the program may 'fall off' the end of the data file while looking for a train. Program 5.12 illustrates a way of doing this. A logical variable TrainFound is used to record that a suitable entry in the timetable has been encountered.

═══════ **PROGRAM 5.11** ═══════

This is an alternative version of Program 5.7 using a variable for one of the loop conditions.

```
/* Program 5.11 : Heat Wave 2 */

#include <stdio.h>
#define FALSE 0
#define TEMP_THRESHOLD 15.0
#define SUN_THRESHOLD 10.0

void main(void)
{
   float NextTemp, NextSun;
   int day;
   int WarmDayFound;

   FILE *WeatherFile;

   day = 0;
   WeatherFile = fopen("WEATHER.DAT", "r");
   WarmDayFound = FALSE;
   do {
     day++;
     fscanf(WeatherFile, "%f%f", &NextTemp, &NextSun);
     WarmDayFound =
         (NextTemp > TEMP_THRESHOLD) &&
         (NextSun  > SUN_THRESHOLD);
   } while ( (day<365) && !WarmDayFound );

   if  ( WarmDayFound )
     {
       printf("There were %i ", day-1);
       printf("days before the first good day.\n");
     }
   else
     printf("That was an exceptionally bad year.\n");

   close(WeatherFile);
}
```

In Program 5.12, we have done something with control structures that we have not done so far: we have used one control structure inside another. In this case, we have used an if statement inside a do loop. This was necessary in order to ensure that we test a timetable entry only if the previous fscanf operation was successful.

This leads us neatly into the main topic of the next chapter.

================== **PROGRAM 5.12** ==================

This is a variation on Program 5.4, but this version detects the end of the timetable
file and reports that no train is available.

```
/* Program 5.12 : Next Train 3*/

#include <stdio.h>
#define FALSE 0

void main(void)
{
   int earliest, depart, arrive;
   int TrainFound;
   FILE *timetable;

   printf("Earliest possible depart time?");   scanf("%i", &earliest);

   timetable = fopen("TIMES.DAT", "r");

   TrainFound = FALSE;
   do {
       fscanf(timetable, "%i%i", &depart, &arrive);
       if (!feof(timetable)) TrainFound = (depart >= earliest);
   } while (!feof(timetable) && !TrainFound);

   if (TrainFound)
   {
      printf("Your train leaves at %i ", depart);
      printf("and arrives at %i\n", arrive);
   }
   else
      printf("No train available.\n");

   fclose(timetable);

}
```

================== SUMMARY OF CHAPTER 5 ==================

Key points

■ A conditional loop tells the computer to repeat an action until some condition no
longer holds.

■ In C, conditional loops are implemented using while and do. The condition itself is a
logical expression.

■ Multiple terminating conditions can be created by using more complex logical expressions, which are constructed using the logical operators.

■ Data terminators remove the requirement that we know in advance how much data will be provided.

■ We can read data from a previously typed text file instead of from the keyboard.

■ If we are reading data from a file, we can test when the end of the file has been reached using `feof`.

Good programming practice

■ Do not use the `for` loop to implement multiple terminating conditions.

■ Any conditional loop can be implemented using `while`, but sometimes the use of a `while` loop is a little more clumsy than a `do` loop.

■ Logical variables allow us to express the terminating condition for a loop, and then test why the loop has terminated.

Common problems	
Problem	**Symptom**
Wrongly placed semicolon immediately after `while(...)` heading.	Loop will execute, doing nothing each time and repeatedly testing the same stopping condition – a (possibly uninterruptable) infinite loop.
`while` condition inverted, for example `while(x>10)` instead of `while(x<10)`.	Loop will probably not execute at all (or only once in the case of a `do` loop).
Attempt to read from a non-existent file.	Program may still attempt to run, producing nonsense.
Opening a file repeatedly in the body of a loop instead of once only outside the loop.	Program will repeatedly read data at the start of the file instead of progressing through the file.
Insufficient data in file.	In the absence of end-of-file tests, the program will continue to run, producing nonsense.
Failure to do correct look-ahead for a data terminator, particularly the end-of-file marker.	Program may not detect the data terminator or the end of a file. The program will either fail or attempt to process data items beyond the terminator.

Debugging tips

- At the start of any suspect loop, use an extra `printf` to print the values of any variables involved in the looping condition.
- Include `printf` statements and additional `feof` tests after suspect `fscanf` statements.

EXERCISES FOR CHAPTER 5

(1) A travelling salesman knows that one of his customers will not be available to see him until after a specified time. He wishes to catch the first train that arrives at the customer's station after that time. Write a program that reads a day's train timetable as used in Program 5.4 and that, given the specified time, tells him when his train leaves. You should find out how to type the timetable into a text file on your system and your program should read the timetable from the file.

(2) An organization has approximately $1000 available to be allocated in small amounts to approved charities. The amounts approved for each charity are to be typed as input for a program in the order in which requests were received. Write a program that will read these amounts and report as soon as over $1000 has been allocated.

check input   Interest is first then payment subtracted

(3) The initial amount of a loan, the monthly repayment and the monthly rate of interest are known. Write a program that will count how many months will elapse before the loan is paid off and print a message indicating the duration of the loan in years and months.

(4) A total of 365 figures representing the rainfall in millimetres for consecutive days in a year are available. Write a program that counts how many days elapsed before the total rainfall for the year up to that point exceeded 250 millimetres. Allow for the possibility of a very dry year.

(5) Write a program that accepts a person's initial bank balance followed by a sequence of positive and negative floating point numbers representing transactions. A positive number represents a credit entry in the account and a negative number represents a debit entry. The input is terminated by a zero entry. The program should print the new balance.

(6) In a board game for three players, the players take turns at making a move, and a player scores a variable number of points for each move made. The game finishes when one of the players obtains a zero score for his or her move. Write a program that accepts, as input, the separate move scores and announces each player's total score. Assume that the scores are supplied to the program three at a time, one for each player in the order in which they played. The last group of scores is to be made up to three, if necessary, by the insertion of one or two additional zeros.

(7) A machine is manufacturing ball bearings and, at equal time intervals during a production run, a ball bearing is sampled and its diameter measured. A sequence of such measurements terminated by a negative number is available for input to a computer program. A similar sequence of measurements is available from a production run on a second machine. Each ball bearing should have a diameter of 2.0 mm. Write a program that reads the two separate sets of measurements and reports which machine is producing samples whose average diameter is closer to the ideal value.

(8) Write a program that accepts as input a set of sample diameter measurements from a production run on one of the machines described in Exercise 7. The program should report whether the sample contained any ball bearings that were excessively large (>2.05) or excessively small (<1.95). The program should not waste time reading further input if such a value is found in the sample.

CHAPTER 6

Statements within statements

Sometimes a control structure needs to be included inside another. For example, it is possible to have a conditional statement inside a loop, a loop within a conditional statement and loops within loops. In this chapter we demonstrate how to write programs involving **nested** control structures. We shall use examples of some of the most commonly occurring structures.

6.1 ■ Conditional statements within loops

We have seen in Chapter 4 that a `for` loop can take the form:

> *for (variable = expression; variable <= expression; variable++)*
>   *statement*

The statement to be obeyed repeatedly can in fact be any C statement (or statement block). We now illustrate the case where an `if` statement is obeyed repeatedly by writing a program to print all of the integers between 2 and 9 that divide exactly into a given integer. We can describe in outline what the program must do, as follows:

```
scanf("%i", &GivenInteger);
for (i = 2; i <= 9; i++)
    Test whether i divides exactly into the given integer;
```

We can now focus our attention on the easier *subproblem* of testing a single value of i. In order to test whether an integer i divides exactly into GivenInteger we can use:

```
if (GivenInteger % i == 0)
    printf("%i divides into %i.\n", i, GivenInteger);
```

and this is the statement that must be repeatedly executed using the `for` statement, as in Program 6.1.

============================= PROGRAM 6.1 =============================

This program prints all of the positive integers under 10 that divide exactly into a given number.

```
/* Program 6.1 : Factors */

#include <stdio.h>

void main(void)
{
    int GivenInteger, i;
    scanf("%i", &GivenInteger);

    for (i = 2; i <= 9; i++)
      if (GivenInteger % i == 0)
        printf("%i divides into %i.\n", i, GivenInteger);

}
```

The `for` statement in Program 6.1 will behave as if a sequence of eight separate `if` statements were obeyed:

```
if (GivenInteger % 2 == 0)
   printf("%i divides into %i.\n", 2, GivenInteger);
if (GivenInteger % 3 == 0)
   printf("%i divides into %i.\n", 3, GivenInteger);
      :
      :
if (GivenInteger % 9 == 0)
   printf("%i divides into %i.\n", 9, GivenInteger);
```

Thus, given input of 18, the program will print:

```
2 divides into 18.
3 divides into 18.
6 divides into 18.
9 divides into 18.
```

In Program 3.1, the same test was applied to three input values by using three separate occurrences of the same `if` statement. Such a process is better structured as a loop:

```
for (count = 1; count <= 3; count++)
   Process the next value in the input
```

The program code to be executed three times can be a compound statement, and it can be as complicated as we like; in this example it must read the next value in the input and then test it as illustrated in Program 6.2.

PROGRAM 6.2

Four numbers are input to this program. The first number is interpreted as a standard value and the three further values are compared with this standard value. A message is printed indicating how many of these three values are within 0.1 of the standard value.

```c
/* Program 6.2 : Tolerance 2 */

#include <stdio.h>
#include <math.h>

void main(void)
{
    float standard, next;
    int NumberClose, count;
    NumberClose = 0;
    scanf("%f", &standard);

    for (count = 1; count <= 3; count++)
    {
        scanf("%f", &next);
        if (fabs(standard - next) < 0.1)
            NumberClose++;
    }

    printf("%i", NumberClose);
    printf(" values are near the standard.\n");

}
```

Program 6.3 is an extension of Program 6.2 to deal with a variable amount of data. In this case the data is terminated by a negative value.

The outline structure is similar to that introduced in Chapter 5, Section 5.6. The first value to be processed is obtained before entering the loop and the next value is always obtained at the end of the loop so that it can be tested for the loop terminating condition before it is processed:

PROGRAM 6.3

This is an elaboration of Program 6.2. Numbers are input to a program from a length measuring device that measures the length of a manufactured component on a production line. The program counts the number of components within 0.1 of a standard length of 6.37 and the number of components outside this tolerance. The program terminates when it receives any negative number. We simulate input from the length measuring device by using scanf and the keyboard.

```c
/* Program 6.3 : Tolerance 3 */

#include <stdio.h>
#include <math.h>
#define STANDARD 6.37

void main(void)
{
    float length;
    int within, without;

    within = 0; without = 0;

    scanf("%f", &length);

    while (length >= 0)
    {
        if (fabs(length - STANDARD) < 0.1)
            within++;
        else
            without++;
        scanf("%f", &length);
    }

    printf("%i values within tolerance.\n", within);
    printf("%i values outside tolerance.\n", without);

}
```

Read the first length to be processed;

```c
while (length >= 0)
{
```

   Test the current length;
   Read the next length to be processed;

```c
}
```

The test required is more elaborate than that in Program 6.2 as we now want to keep two counts – values within the tolerance and values outside the tolerance.

Program 6.4 simulates the behaviour of a coin-operated vending machine. The outline structure in this case is:

```
do
    Process the next coin;

while (total < 123);
```

PROGRAM 6.4

This is a program that is to control a coin-operated vending machine. We assume that coins of denomination 50, 20, 10, 5, 2 and 1 have weights of 35, 19, 16, 9, 7 and 3, respectively. Also, we are simulating a single coin being put in the slot by scanf("%i",&weight). The program is to print a message as soon as at least £1.23 has been inserted, calculating any change due.

```
/* Program 6.4 : Coins */
#include <stdio.h>
void main(void)
{
    int weight, total;
    total = 0;
    do {
        scanf("%i", &weight);
        switch (weight)
        {
            case 35: total += 50; break;
            case 16: total += 10; break;
            case 19: total += 20; break;
            case  9: total += 5;  break;
            case  7: total += 2;  break;
            case  3: total++;     break;
            default: printf("Coin rejected\n");
        }
    } while (total < 123);
    printf("Coins accepted.\n");
    if (total > 123)
        printf("Change due: %i\n", total - 123);
}
```

The solution to the subproblem of processing a single coin uses a `switch` statement and was used as an example in Chapter 3, Section 3.7. The C code for this is inserted inside the `do` loop as illustrated in the completed version of Program 6.4.

6.2 ■ Loops within loops

One loop inside another loop is a nested structure frequently encountered in programs. This is because so much data analysed by computer programs is organized in the form of tables.

Consider the problem of processing the five examination marks obtained by each of 25 candidates. The structure required is a loop of the form:

```
for (candidate = 1; candidate <= 25; candidate++)
```
Process the marks obtained by the candidate

Processing one candidate's marks might involve reading the five marks obtained, computing the average and testing for a pass or fail:

```
total = 0;
for (exam = 1; exam <= 5; exam++)
{
   scanf("%i", &mark);
   total += mark;
}
average = total / 5.0;
printf("Candidate %i", candidate);
printf(" - Average mark: %.1f ", average);
if (average >= 50)
   printf(" [Pass]\n");
else
   printf(" [Fail]\n");
```

and a segment of program like this must be obeyed 25 times. This can be achieved by bracketing it into a single compound statement and inserting it into the previous `for` statement, giving Program 6.5.

At this point, indentation becomes even more important than ever. A program is typed only once, but it will be read many times by the programmer when testing it or making alterations to it, and it may also be read by other people who wish to understand the techniques that the programmer has used. Good indentation can make it much easier to understand the control structure of the program. Thus, in Program 6.5, the body of the `exam` loop has been indented to make it stand out from the body of the `candidate` loop, which has in turn been indented to make it stand out from the rest of the program.

In Program 6.5 the outer loop is executed 25 times. Once the computer enters the innermost loop, it stays there until this loop has been executed five times. The innermost instructions are executed a total of 25 × 5 times, and 125 marks would be

============ PROGRAM 6.5 ============

Data is presented to this program in the form of a table. The table consists of 25 rows
of five exam marks, each row representing the performance of one candidate in five
exams. The program outputs a reference number, a pass/fail message and an average
mark for each of the 25 candidates.

```
/* Program 6.5 : Exam Marks */
#include <stdio.h>
void main(void)
{
   int candidate, exam, total, mark;
   float average;
   for (candidate = 1; candidate <= 25; candidate++)
   {
      total = 0;
      for (exam = 1; exam <= 5; exam++)
      {
         scanf("%i", &mark);
         total += mark;
      }
      average = total / 5.0;
      printf("Candidate %i", candidate);
      printf(" - Average mark: %.1f ", average);
      if (average >= 50)
         printf(" [Pass]\n");
      else
         printf(" [Fail]\n");
   }
}
```

supplied as input data in the form of 25 groups of five marks. If we imagine a counter
associated with each loop then the exam counter would be turning five times as fast
as the candidate counter, resetting to 1 for each new candidate.

outer loop
candidate = 1
                        inner loop
                            exam = 1
                                   2
                                   3
                                   4
                                   5

```
candidate = 2
                    inner loop
                            exam = 1
                                   2
                                   3
                                   4
                                   5

        .
        .
        .
candidate = 25
                    inner loop
                            exam = 1
                                   2
                                   3
                                   4
                                   5
```

To improve your understanding of the idea of a nested loop, you should examine the difference in behaviour between the following two fragments of program:

```
for (i = 1; i <= 3; i++)
   for (j = 1; j <=3; j++)
      printf("%i %i\n", i, j);
```

which prints:

```
1 1
1 2
1 3
2 1
2 2
2 3
3 1
3 2
3 3
```

and:

```
for (i = 1; i <= 3; i++)
   printf("%i\n", i);

for (j = 1; j <= 3; j++)
   printf("%i\n", j);
```

which prints:

```
1
2
3
1
2
3
```

The first fragment is, of course, a nested structure, whereas the second is just two consecutive loops. As a further illustration, let us construct a program that will display a triangle of stars (of a given size) on a background of dots. For example a triangle of four lines would be:

```
.........
....*....
...***...
..*****..
.*******.
.........
```

In outline, the program required will behave as follows:

```
scanf ("%i", &rows);
```
Calculate width of picture;
```
for (count = 1; count <= WidthOfPicture; count++)
    printf(".");
printf("\n");

for(row = 1; row <= rows; row++)
{
```
  Print the next row of the triangle with
  the appropriate number of dots on each side;
```
}

for (count = 1; count <= WidthOfPicture; count++)
    printf(".");
printf("\n");
```

The width of the picture is given by `2*rows + 1`. Printing a row of the triangle can be described in more detail as:

Calculate number of stars in this row;
Calculate number of background dots at each end of row;
```
for (count = 1; count <= dots; count++) printf(".");
for (count = 1; count <= stars; count++) printf("*");
for (count = 1; count <= dots; count++) printf(".");
```

The number of stars to be printed on a row is `2*row - 1` and the number of background dots required is `rows + 1 - row`. These loops must be nested inside the second loop in the outline above because our triangle is made up of a number of such lines. Filling in these details, we get Program 6.6.

The final example in this section involves an `if` statement inside a `do` loop inside a `for` loop.

Part of a daily sales analysis program involves printing a list of the number of items costing more than $10 that were sold in each of 63 departments:

```
for (dept = 1; dept <= 63; dept++)
```
  Analyse the sales for one department

PROGRAM 6.6

This program displays a triangle of stars of a specified height on a background of dots.

```
/* Program 6.6 : Framed Triangle */
#include <stdio.h>
void main(void)
{
   int rows, WidthOfPicture, count,
       row, stars, dots;
   printf("\nheight of triangle:");  scanf("%i", &rows);
   WidthOfPicture = 2*rows + 1;
   printf("\n");
   for (count = 1; count <= WidthOfPicture; count++)
      printf(".");
   printf("\n");
   for(row = 1; row <= rows; row++)
   { stars = 2*row - 1;
      dots  = rows + 1 - row;
      for (count = 1; count <= dots; count++) printf(".");
      for (count = 1; count <= stars; count++) printf("*");
      for (count = 1; count <= dots; count++) printf(".");
      printf("\n");
   }
   for (count = 1; count <= WidthOfPicture; count++)
      printf(".");
   printf("\n");
}
```

The input for each department consists of a list containing the price of each item sold in the department on the day in question, and each list is terminated by -1. One department's sales can therefore be analysed by:

```
LargeSales = 0;
scanf("%f", &NextItemPrice);
while (NextItemPrice >= 0.0)
{
```
Test NextItemPrice to see if it is a large sale;
```
   scanf("%f", &NextItemPrice);
}
```
Print the number of large sales for this department;

Filling in the rest of the details, we obtain Program 6.7. This program could, of course, be made to take its data from a file by using the file handling facilities introduced in Chapter 5, Section 5.3.

════════════════ **PROGRAM 6.7** ════════════════

```
/* Program 6.7 : Sales Analysis */
#include <stdio.h>

void main(void)
{
   int dept, LargeSales;
   float NextItemPrice;

   for (dept = 1; dept <= 63; dept++)
   { LargeSales = 0;
     scanf("%f", &NextItemPrice);

     while (NextItemPrice >= 0.0)
     {
        if (NextItemPrice >= 10.0)
           LargeSales++;
        scanf("%f", &NextItemPrice);
     }

     printf("Department %i has made ", dept);
     printf("%i large sales.\n", LargeSales);

   }

}
```

6.3 ■ Nested if statements

Consider the following sequence of three if statements:

```
if (age < 21)
   printf("Refuse policy\n");

if (age >= 35)
   printf("Issue policy with discount\n");

if ((age >= 21) && (age < 35))
   printf("Issue policy at full price\n");
```

Here three consecutive if statements are used to select one of three possible courses of action. The three conditions used are such that one and only one of them must be TRUE. However, even if the condition in the first if statement is TRUE, the computer will still waste time testing the conditions in the remaining two if statements.

If the conditions in the first two if statements are FALSE, the condition in the third must be TRUE and the computer will again waste time testing it. These inefficiencies can be eliminated by using a more appropriate if statement structure for making the tests involved. Let us start by noting that if age < 21 then the first printf statement should be obeyed and no further tests made. This can be achieved by using an if-else structure that can be outlined as follows:

```
if (age < 21)
   printf("Refuse policy\n");
else
      Statement to be obeyed only if age >= 21;
```

Any statement inserted after the else will be obeyed only if age >= 21. In this example we can obtain the effect we require by making the statement after the else a further if statement which distinguishes the cases age >= 35 and age < 35:

```
if (age < 21)
   printf("Refuse policy\n");
else
   if (age >= 35)
     printf("Issue policy with discount\n");
   else
     printf("Issue policy at full price\n");
```

This version of the program will not test the second condition if the first is satisfied and will automatically obey the third printf statement if the first two conditions are FALSE. We can illustrate the behaviour of this nested if statement as shown in Figure 6.1. We can imagine the computer following one path from the top of this diagram and carrying out the action at the end of that path.

You should now compare the structure of Program 6.8 with that of Program 3.7, which is identical in effect, and by constructing a tree diagram appreciate the difference between the two structures.

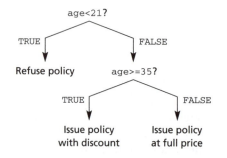

Figure 6.1 The behaviour of a nested if statement.

====== **PROGRAM 6.8** ======

This is a more efficient version of Program 3.7, which selected one out of eight messages to be displayed according to three items of information input – age, size of car and conviction record.

```c
/* Program 6.8 : Insurance Policy 2 */

#include <stdio.h>

#define P45 "Policy loaded by 45 per cent.\n"
#define P15 "Policy loaded by 15 per cent.\n"
#define P30 "Policy loaded by 30 per cent.\n"
#define OK  "No loading.\n"
#define NO  "No policy to be issued.\n"
#define P60 "Policy loaded by 60 per cent.\n"
#define P50 "Policy loaded by 50 per cent.\n"
#define P10 "Policy loaded by 10 per cent.\n"

void main(void)
{
  int over21, LargeCar, RiskDriver;
  int age, cc, convictions;

  scanf("%i%i%i", &age, &cc, &convictions);
  over21 = (age >= 21);
  LargeCar = (cc >= 2000);
  RiskDriver = (convictions >= 3);

  if (over21)
  {
    if (LargeCar) {
      if (RiskDriver) printf(P45);
      else printf(P15); }
    else {
      if (RiskDriver) printf(P30);
      else printf(OK); }
  }
  else
  {
    if (LargeCar) {
      if (RiskDriver) printf(NO);
      else printf(P60); }
    else {
      if (RiskDriver) printf(P50);
      else printf(P10); }
  }
}
```

Program 6.9 illustrates the use of a nested `if` statement within a loop. It uses the same outline structure as for Program 6.3:

Read the first length to be processed;

```
while (length >= 0)
{
```

    Test the current length;
    Read the next length to be processed;

```
}
```

PROGRAM 6.9

This is a further elaboration of Program 6.3. The program counts the number of components within 0.1 of a standard length of 6.37, the number of components whose length is too high and the number whose length is too low.

```c
/* Program 6.9 : Tolerance 4 */
#include <stdio.h>
#include <math.h>
#define STANDARD 6.37
void main(void)
{
   float length;
   int above, below, within;

   within = 0; above = 0;
   below = 0; scanf("%f", &length);

   while (length >= 0)
   {
      if (fabs(length - STANDARD) < 0.1)
         within++;
      else
         if ( (length - STANDARD) >= 0.1)
            above++;
         else
            below++;
      scanf("%f", &length);

   }
   printf("%i values are within tolerance.\n", within);
   printf("%i values are too large.\n", above);
   printf("%i values are too small.\n", below);

}
```

To test a length, we now require to distinguish three separate possibilities as follows:

```
if (fabs(length - STANDARD) < 0.1)
   within++;
else
   if ( (length - STANDARD) >= 0.1)
      above++;
   else
      below++;
```

We finish this section by drawing your attention to a minor difficulty that can arise when nesting if statements, some of which have no else part. The computer always assumes that an else belongs to the nearest unterminated if. Thus, in a statement such as:

```
if (condition1)
   if (condition2) printf("Statement1 executed\n");
   else printf("Statement2 executed\n");
```

the else belongs to the second if and the computer will behave as shown in Figure 6.2.

For example, when the computer obeys the statement:

```
if (x > 50)
   if (y > 50) printf("both values > 50\n");
   else printf("Only the first value is > 50\n");
```

no action at all is taken if x <= 50.

If necessary, braces can be used to terminate an if statement as follows:

```
if (condition1)
{
   if (condition2) printf("Statement1 executed\n");
}
else printf("Statement2 executed\n");
```

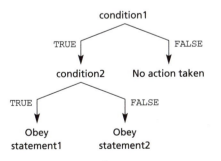

Figure 6.2 Showing the problem that can arise when some nested if statements have no else part.

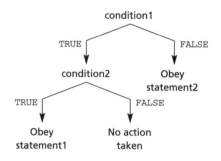

Figure 6.3 The effect of using braces to enclose a nested `if` statement with no `else` part.

The braces indicate that the enclosed `if` statement is complete and the following `else` is taken as belonging to the first `if`. In this case the computer behaves as shown in Figure 6.3.

For example, if the computer obeys the statement:

```
if (x > 50)
{
   if (y > 50) printf("both values > 50\n");
}
else printf("The first value is not > 50\n");
```

no action is taken if `x > 50` and `y <= 50`.

6.4 ■ Data validation: Guarding a program

When it is possible to check or **validate** the data input to a program this should always be done. Not only does this guard against the possibility of an execution error, the cause of which might not be immediately apparent, but worse – invalid data may cause erroneous results which go unnoticed. In simple cases, we can use a structure such as:

Read data;
```
if (data is ok)
{
```
   Main part of program
```
}
else
```
   Print an error message;

Program 6.10 uses this structure.

PROGRAM 6.10

This program calculates the cost of a holiday by multiplying the duration in days by a daily rate that is seasonally dependent. The input data is two dates in the form day, month, and we assume that the months are either going to be identical or consecutive. Also, we assume that it is the second month that determines the seasonal rate.

```c
/* Program 6.10 : Holiday */

#include <stdio.h>
#define LOWRATE  100
#define MIDRATE  200
#define PEAKRATE 300

void main(void)
{
    int day1, month1, day2, month2;
    int duration, TillEndOfMonth, cost;

    scanf("%i%i", &day1, &month1);
    scanf("%i%i", &day2, &month2);

    if ( (day1 >= 1) && (day1 <= 31) &&
         (day2 >= 1) && (day2 <= 31) &&
         (month1 >= 1) && (month1 <= 12) &&
         (month2 >= 1) && (month2 <= 12) &&
         (month1 <= month2) )

    {
        if (month1 == month2)
            duration = day2 - day1 + 1;
        else
        {
            switch(month1)
            {
                case 2  :
                    TillEndOfMonth = 28 - day1; break;
                case 9  : case 4: case 6: case 11:
                    TillEndOfMonth = 30 - day1; break;
                default :
                    TillEndOfMonth = 31 - day1;
            }
            duration = day2 + TillEndOfMonth + 1;
        }
    }
```

```
    switch(month2) {
       case 1: case 2: case 11: case 12:
          cost = duration * LOWRATE; break;
       case 3: case 4: case 5: case 10:
          cost = duration * MIDRATE; break;
       case 6: case 7: case 8: case 9:
          cost = duration * PEAKRATE; break;
    }
    printf("Cost of holiday is $%i\n", cost);
 }
 else printf("You have typed erroneous dates.\n");
}
```

In Program 6.10 we have simplified the input data check (not every month has 31 days and if one value is wrong all four have to be retyped); but comprehensive validation would be too lengthy for the purpose of this demonstration. The innermost block is entered only if the data is acceptable (within the limits of the test used). If the data is erroneous the computer will have to be told to execute the program again. If a program is required to request automatically more input until a correct set of data values have been typed, then the following structure can be used:

Read data;
while (*data is faulty*)
{
    Write a message requesting data to be retyped;
    Read data;
}
Main part of program;

In the case of Program 6.10, use of this structure would give us:

```
scanf("%i%i", &day1, &month1);
scanf("%i%i", &day2, &month2);

while (!( (day1 >= 1) && (day1 <= 31) &&
          (day2 >= 1) && (day2 <= 31) &&
          (month1 >= 1) && (month1 <= 12) &&
          (month2 >= 1) && (month2 <= 12) &&
          (month1 <= month2) ) )
```

```
{
    printf("Error in dates - please retype.\n");
    scanf("%i%i", &day1, &month1);
    scanf("%i%i", &day2, &month2);
}
```

Calculation part of program;

It would be easier to rearrange this second structure and have four input and test loops, one for each item of data.

6.5 ▩ Stepwise refinement

In writing some of the programs in this chapter, we have informally introduced the technique that is sometimes termed **stepwise refinement** or **top-down program design**. Instead of attempting to write down a complete C program in one step, we first decide what the outermost control structure in the program should be. For example, in writing Program 6.7, we can see immediately that there are 63 separate sales analyses to be made. Giving a brief English description to the process of analysing one department's sales enabled us to write down an outline of this loop:

```
for (dept = 1; dept <= 63; dept++)
```
    Analyse the sales for one department

Having got this clear in our minds, we then concentrated on the rather easier **subproblem** of analysing one department's sales, and the code for doing this was eventually inserted in the above structure. This subproblem was of course tackled by a further application of stepwise refinement.

Such an approach enables the construction of a complex nested control structure to be broken down into a number of simpler programming tasks that are more or less independent of each other. This is just one aspect of the set of programming techniques known as **structured programming**.

In the Introduction, we mentioned the use of methodologies for the specification, design and implementation of large software projects. Some of the main stages involved might be:

▪ Careful and detailed specification of what the program is to do. This specification can be written carefully in English or in one of the mathematical specification languages that have been developed for the purpose. This specification may even have the status of a legally binding contract between the program developers and a client.

■ Design of the structure of the program required to implement the specification. This stage will often use specialized techniques for analysing the structure of the data involved and mapping these to the control structures required. Many of the methodologies use pictorial notations to help with the design process.

■ Writing the code in C or some other programming language. This stage should be easy provided the previous stage has been done correctly and in sufficient detail.

A detailed discussion of these techniques is beyond the scope of this book, and for the level of difficulty of the examples we will look at, a simple stepwise refinement approach will be adequate. In the next chapter, we explore stepwise refinement further and introduce ways of giving names to subprograms. This will enable us to structure our C code in a way that matches the structure of the design process used to create the code.

SUMMARY OF CHAPTER 6

Key points

■ Sometimes one control structure needs to be included inside another.

■ When dealing with tables of data, one `for` loop nested within another is often an appropriate control structure.

■ When a process operates on data which is expected to satisfy certain conditions, we can protect that part of the program by nesting it inside an `if` statement. If the data provided is not in the correct format or falls outside the desired range, an alternative course of action can be taken. This is sometimes known as **data validation**.

■ **Stepwise refinement** consists of first deciding what the outmost control structure must be, and then tackling the remaining subproblem (it too may need to be broken down). This is also known as **top-down program design**.

Good programming practice

■ Consecutive `if` statements can lead to inefficiencies. One `if` statement nested within another can save evaluating the same condition twice.

■ Mixing `if` statements and `if-else` statements can lead to problems – clarify your intentions with braces.

■ Indentation is more important than ever in order to make clear the control structure of a program.

Common problems	
Problem	**Symptom**
Failure to analyse clearly the structure of the control statements required.	Program will fail completely, or will attempt to process data in the wrong order, or will produce output in the wrong order.
Failure to position braces correctly (especially closing braces).	Program control structure will differ from that intended – symptoms as above.

Debugging tips

- Place extra `printf` statements to print values of key variables at the start of each of the main control structures, particularly at the start of loops and at the start of the branches of large `if` statements.
- If the program is clearly divided into stages, print out main variables between stages.
- Use indentation and carefully line up braces to make obvious the nested structure of the program.

EXERCISES FOR CHAPTER 6

(1) Given input data consisting of 30 numbers, some of which are positive and some negative, write a program that finds the average of the positive numbers and the average of the negative numbers.

(2) Write a program that accepts as input a set of sample diameter readings from one of the ball bearing machines described in Exercise 7, Chapter 5. A ball bearing is classified as faulty if its diameter is less than 1.99 mm or greater than 2.01 mm. Your program should report the percentage of faulty ball bearings in the sample.

Now extend your program to accept two successive sets of readings from two machines and to report which machine is producing the smaller proportion of faulty samples.

(3) Write a program that accepts as input data two numbers representing the width and height of a rectangle. The program is then to print such a rectangle made up of asterisks, for example:

```
* * * * * *
* * * * * *
* * * * * *
```

(4) Write a program to accept a single integer and print a multiplication table for all of the positive integers up to the one specified as input.

(5) Write a program that will read the lengths of three sides of a triangle (three integers) and print the lengths of the sides in descending order followed by a message to say whether the triangle is right-angled.

(6) Extend your solution to Exercise 5 to include a test to check that the data does in fact specify a legal triangle. (The sum of the two smallest sides must be greater than the largest side.)

(7) The monthly life insurance premium charged by an insurance company is dependent on the age of the applicant. A basic premium of $5 is charged but this may be subject to one or more $2 increments. Only applicants who will not be 65 or over on their next birthday are eligible and the number of increments is determined by the applicant's age as follows:

Age next birthday	Increments
< 20	0
>= 21 and < 30	1
>= 30 and < 45	2
>= 45 and < 65	3

Write a program to print the monthly premium for an applicant. The data input is date-of-birth and current-date, each as three integers.

(8) Write a program that accepts as input the numbers of two months (in the same year) followed by the number of the year, and outputs the total number of days from the beginning of the first month to the end of the second month.

(9) Extend your solution to Exercise 8 so that it accepts two dates in the form, for example:

```
13   6
25   12
```

where the first number in each pair is a day and the second is a month. Again assume that both dates are in the same year. The dates will be followed in the input by the number of the year. The program should print the number of days from the first date to the second date.

CHAPTER 7

Giving a process
a name

In Chapter 6, we introduced, informally, the technique of structured programming. This involved identifying subprocesses of the original problem, which could then be further developed independently. In C, we can give names to sections of a program and write the name wherever that section of program is to be obeyed. Giving names to clearly identifiable sections can make large programs easier for ourselves and other people to read. In C a named section of program is called a **function**, and functions are used extensively throughout the rest of the book. In this Chapter we introduce the basic ideas. The functions introduced in Sections 7.1–7.3 are usually called **procedures** in other programming languages. They are not true functions in the mathematical sense – there is no returned function value. However, the term 'procedure' is not usually used by C programmers. In C, a procedure is treated as a function that does not produce any result and is usually referred to as a **void function**.

7.1 ■ Simple void functions

The first example illustrates how a void function could be used in Program 6.5. Recall that the outline structure developed for this program was:

```
for (candidate = 1; candidate <= 25; candidate++)
    Process the marks obtained by the candidate
```

Processing the marks for one candidate was a much easier subproblem than the original problem and was implemented by the program fragment:

```
total = 0;
for (exam = 1; exam <= 5; exam++)
{
    scanf("%i", &mark);
    total += mark;
}
```

```
average = total / 5.0;
printf("Candidate %i", candidate);
printf(" - Average mark: %.1f ", average);

if (average >= 50)
  printf(" [Pass]\n");
else
  printf(" [Fail]\n");
```

Instead of simply writing this complete piece of text into the loop where it is to be executed, we can give it a name, ProcessCandidate, say. The main loop then appears more or less as it did in our outline program design:

```
for (candidate = 1; candidate <= 25; candidate++)
  ProcessCandidate();
```

and the operation called ProcessCandidate is defined separately. The complete program is presented as Program 7.1.

There are a number of points to note:

- The definition of ProcessCandidate is constructed in the same way as the definition of the main function.
- The definition of ProcessCandidate appears at the end of the program after it has been used in the main function.
- ProcessCandidate is declared briefly at the start of the program before it is used in the main function. This would not have been necessary if we had placed the full definition of ProcessCandidate before the main function, but this would not have reflected the order in which we developed the program. Notice that the introductory declaration is terminated by a semicolon, whereas the heading that introduces the full definition is not. This introductory declaration is usually referred to as a **function prototype**.
- The variables exam, mark and total are declared within the definition of ProcessCandidate and can only be referred to from inside that function. They are said to be **local** to the function.
- The variable candidate was declared at the head of the program and is **global** – it can be referred to from anywhere in the program.

7.2 ■ Void functions with parameters

Previously, we introduced the idea of a void function as a way of naming a section of program. We also saw that a C function can have its own local variables which are inaccessible to the rest of the program. In the examination mark example

═════════════ **PROGRAM 7.1** ═════════════

This is version of Program 6.5 using a void function to emphasize the logical structure of the program.

```
/* Program 7.1 : Exam Marks 2 */
#include <stdio.h>

void ProcessCandidate(void);

int candidate;

void main(void)
{
   for (candidate = 1; candidate <= 25; candidate++)
      ProcessCandidate();

}

void ProcessCandidate(void)
{ int exam, mark, total;
   float average;

      total = 0;
      for (exam = 1; exam <= 5; exam++)
      {
         scanf("%i", &mark);
         total += mark;
      }
      average = total / 5.0;
      printf("Candidate %i", candidate);
      printf(" - Average mark: %.1f ", average);
      if (average >= 50)
         printf(" [Pass]\n");
      else
         printf(" [Fail]\n");

}
```

presented, there was also a global variable, candidate. As a general rule, it is good
programming practice to make functions as self-contained as possible and avoid
the use of such global variables. This decreases the possibility of using the same
variable for conflicting purposes in separate functions. In the examination mark
example, this presents a difficulty as the value of the candidate variable is required
in the function ProcessCandidate as well as in the main function. The solution
to this dilemma is to use a **parameter** to communicate this value to the
ProcessCandidate function, as illustrated in Program 7.2.

━━━━━━━━━━━━━━━━━━━━━━━ **PROGRAM 7.2** ━━━━━━━━━━━━━━━━━━━━━

Examination marks again – using a parameter.

```
/* Program 7.2 : Exam Marks 3 */
#include <stdio.h>

void ProcessCandidate(int cand);

void main(void)
{
  int candidate;
  for (candidate = 1; candidate <= 25; candidate++)
    ProcessCandidate(candidate);

}

void ProcessCandidate(int cand)
{ int exam, mark, total;
  float average;

    total = 0;
    for (exam = 1; exam <= 5; exam++)
    {
      scanf("%i", &mark);
      total += mark;
    }
    average = total / 5.0;
    printf("Candidate %i", cand);
    printf(" - Average mark: %.1f ", average);
    if (average >= 50)
      printf(" [Pass]\n");
    else
      printf(" [Fail]\n");

}
```

- The heading for the function now includes the declaration of an integer
  parameter in parentheses. A parameter used in a function definition is
  usually called a **dummy** parameter or a **formal** parameter. The word
  'argument' is often used in C instead of the word 'parameter'.
- When the function is called, any dummy parameters in the function
  definition have to be given actual values. An **actual parameter** has to be
  supplied in parentheses after the name of the function. In this case the value
  supplied is the value of the variable candidate.

■ The variable `candidate` is now declared at the start of the `main` function and can only be referred to inside the `main` function. The function `ProcessCandidate` no longer needs to access this variable, since the value required is passed to it via the parameter.

A value could have been supplied to the function in a variety of ways. For example, if there had been only three candidates, we could have called the function from `main` three times without bothering with a loop:

```
ProcessCandidate(1);
ProcessCandidate(2);
ProcessCandidate(3);
```

Any expression can be used that evaluates to the type of value required by the function. A rather eccentric, but equally valid, version of the above would be:

```
ProcessCandidate(54-53);
ProcessCandidate(84/2-40);
ProcessCandidate(9/3);
```

Program 7.3 contains an example of a function with three parameters.

PROGRAM 7.3

Two well-known mathematical constants are called π and e. Tabulate powers of π (=3.14159) from 3 to 6 and powers of e (=2.71828) from 2 to 7.

```
/* Program 7.3 : Powers */

#include <stdio.h>
#include <math.h>
#define pi 3.14159
#define e 2.71828

void PrintPowers(float x, int p1, int p2);

void main(void)
{
   PrintPowers(pi, 3,6);
   PrintPowers(e,  2,7);
}

void PrintPowers(float x, int p1, int p2)
{ int p;
   printf("\n\nPowers of %.5f\n\n  n    pow(%.5f,n)\n",x,x);
   for (p = p1; p <= p2; p++)
      printf("%3i        %10.5f\n", p, pow(x,p));
}
```

The function PrintPowers is defined in terms of three parameters called x, p1 and p2. The type of each parameter has to be specified separately in the function heading, with commas separating them. When the function is called, the actual values for the parameters are listed in the same order as in the function heading, and are also separated by commas. These values are then used in place of the corresponding dummy parameters when obeying the body of the function.

Program 7.4 is an example in which we have used two functions. Note the use of the keyword long before our int declarations in this program. A long int behaves just like an int, but it allows storage of much larger numbers.

In attempting to write a program like Program 7.4, or in attempting to understand a program that someone else has written, always remember to start with the main function. Once this has been dealt with, any functions called in main can be treated in the same way, then any functions called by these functions, and so on. In this case, the main body of the program is straightforward, provided that we avoid getting bogged down in the problems involved in printing a number with the commas inserted. Designing the function CommaWrite can then be viewed as a programming problem that is rather easier than the original problem. The need for the function ZeroWrite arises because, for example, a number of thousands has to be written with a full three digits in the context of a number like 2,067,003. In the number 67,003 the thousands are printed with no extra zeros, and a normal printf statement is used. Now read through the above program in this way and ensure that you understand it.

Actually there is a special formatting code in C that does away with the need for defining ZeroWrite. We used it in Program 2.5. The nested if statement in CommaWrite could have been rewritten as:

```
if (millions > 0)
   printf("%i,%03i,%03i", millions, thousands, units);
else
   if (thousands > 0)
      printf("%i,%03i", thousands, units);
   else printf("%i", units);
```

The format code %03i says that an integer should be printed occupying three character positions, and that zeros should be inserted, if necessary, rather than spaces.

7.3 ■ Reference parameters

In the functions of the previous section, a parameter was always used for specifying a **value** which was to be processed when the function was called. As another example of this, consider the following function definition:

```
void process(int x)
{
   printf("%i\n", x);
   printf("%i\n", x*x);
   printf("\n");
}
```

========= **PROGRAM 7.4** =========

This program reads two positive integers and prints them in descending order. The integers are to be output on separate lines and, when an integer is output, the millions are to be followed by a comma and the thousands are to be followed by a comma. Thus, instead of writing 5674251 the program should write 5,674,251.

```c
/* Program 7.4 : Compare */

#include <stdio.h>

void CommaWrite(long int n);
void ZeroWrite(int m);

void main(void)
{ long int first, second;
  scanf("%li%li", &first, &second);
  if (first > second)
  { CommaWrite(first); CommaWrite(second); }
  else
  { CommaWrite(second); CommaWrite(first); }
}

void CommaWrite(long int n)
{ int millions, thousands, units;
  millions = (n / 1000000);
  thousands = (n % 1000000) / 1000;
  units = (n % 1000);

  if (millions > 0)
  { printf("%i,", millions);
    ZeroWrite(thousands); putchar(',');
    ZeroWrite(units);
  }
  else
  { if (thousands > 0)
    { printf("%i,", thousands);
      ZeroWrite(units);
    }
    else printf("%i", units);
  }
  printf("\n");
}

void ZeroWrite(int m)
{
  if (m < 100) printf("0");
  if (m < 10) printf("0");
  printf("%i", m);
}
```

When this function is called, the parameter corresponding to x can be any expression representing an integer value. For example, provided that the variable a contains an integer value, then each of the following statements is a valid call of this function:

```
process(6);
process(a);
process(a*5 + 32);
```

When a function is called, a simple parameter can be used only for transferring information *into* the function. We sometimes need to use a parameter to transfer information *out of* the function back to the calling section of the program. This is done by giving the function a **reference** parameter that tells the function where to put the required information. Let us return to the vote counting example used in Chapter 5, Program 5.10. We shall extend this program to print a message indicating who has won the election. An outline of what the program must do is as follows:

Add up the votes for one party and put the total in Party1Overall;
Add up the votes for the other party and put the total in Party2Overall;

```
if (Party1Overall == Party2Overall)
    printf("A draw.\n");
else if (Party1Overall > Party2Overall)
    printf("A win for party 1.\n");
else
    printf("A win for party 2.\n");
```

Clearly, the two processes involved in the first section of the above outline are similar. In the first case, we want to read and add numbers, placing the total in the variable Party1Overall, and in the second case, we want to perform exactly the same operation except that the total is to be placed in Party2Overall. We shall define a function AddUpVotesFor, which can be used as follows:

```
AddUpVotesFor(&Party1Overall);
AddUpVotesFor(&Party2Overall);
```

Note the use of the & symbol before the name of the parameter in each function call. Here, we require the function to place a value in a *variable* that is supplied as a parameter when the function is called. The function is being given a reference to the variable. We have already seen the use of the & operator in scanf for exactly the same reason – scanf places any values it reads into variables and has to be given references to these variables rather than their values.

In the function definition, we must indicate that the function expects to be given a reference rather than a value. In general, if a function is to be called with the intention of changing one of its parameters by assigning a value to that parameter or by reading a value into it, then that parameter must be declared with an asterisk (*) before the parameter name in the function heading.

In fact, when we place & before a variable name in a function call, it causes the *address* of that variable to be passed to the function. For this reason & is often called the **addressing operator**. The address of a variable is a number (whose actual value we need not concern ourselves with) telling the computer where in its memory to find that variable. The concept of addresses, or **pointers** as they are usually called, becomes an important one in more advanced C.

The complete vote counting program appears as Program 7.5. When AddUpVotesFor is called by:

```
AddUpVotesFor(&Party1Overall);
```

━━━━━━━━━━━━━━━━━━━━━━ **PROGRAM 7.5** ━━━━━━━━━━━━━━━━━━━━

This is Program 5.10 rewritten to use a function and to test who has won the election.

```
/* Program 7.5 : Election 3 */

#include <stdio.h>

void AddUpVotesFor(int *total);

void main(void)
{ int Party1Overall, Party2Overall;

   AddUpVotesFor(&Party1Overall);
   AddUpVotesFor(&Party2Overall);

   if (Party1Overall == Party2Overall)
      printf("A draw.\n");
   else if (Party1Overall > Party2Overall)
      printf("A win for party 1.\n");
   else
      printf("A win for party 2.\n");
}

void AddUpVotesFor(int *total)
{
   int next;
   *total = 0;
   scanf("%i", &next);
   do {
      *total += next;
      scanf("%i", &next);
   } while (next >= 0);
}
```

the function expects a reference to an integer, and is obeyed with `total` referring to the address of `Party1Overall`. When we want to change the value of the variable at that address, we again need an asterisk before the parameter name, as in the statement:

```
*total = 0;
```

which (in the case of the function call we are discussing) sets the value of `Party1Overall` to zero. The * operator is called the **dereferencing operator**. Whenever the statement:

```
*total += next;
```

is obeyed, the computer behaves on this occasion as if it was obeying:

```
Party1Overall += next;
```

The result of obeying the function on this occasion is to add up the first set of votes supplied as input, the total being accumulated in `Party1Overall`. Later, when the function is obeyed as a result of:

```
AddUpVotesFor(&Party2Overall);
```

each reference to `*total` behaves like a reference to `Party2Overall`. This call of the function thus adds up the second set of votes in the input, accumulating the total in `Party2Overall`.

It would clearly be *wrong* for a call of the function `AddUpVotesFor` to have a constant or expression as its parameter:

```
AddUpVotesFor(3);
AddUpVotesFor(Party1Overall + Party2Overall);
```

The function expects to be told *where to put* a value and must therefore be given the address of a variable as its actual parameter.

There is no reason why a function should not be supplied with a reference to a variable that already has a value stored in it. Any such value may be operated on during the execution of the function. As an example, we shall write a program that reads three numbers and prints them in descending order. To do this, the numbers will be read and stored in the order in which they are input in three variables: `first`, `second` and `third`. The program will then rearrange the numbers as follows:

Order the two numbers in `first` *and* `second`*;*
```
/* this may involve swapping their contents */
```
Order the two numbers now in `first` *and* `third`*;*
```
/* "first" now contains the largest number */
```
Order the two numbers now in `second` *and* `third`

We shall define a function that will examine the contents of two specified variables and, if necessary, swap their contents so as to ensure that the larger number is in the first variable and the smaller number is in the other. This function will be used as follows:

```
order(&first, &second);
order(&first, &third);
order(&second, &third);
```

The complete program is given as Program 7.6.

PROGRAM 7.6

This program reads three numbers and prints them in descending order.

```
/* Program 7.6 : Sort 3 numbers */

#include <stdio.h>

void order(int *a, int *b);

void main(void)
{ int first, second, third;

    scanf("%i%i%i", &first, &second, &third);
    order(&first, &second);
    order(&first, &third);
    order(&second, &third);
    printf("%6i%6i%6i\n", first, second, third);
}

void order(int *a, int *b)
{
    int temp;
    if (*a < *b)
    {
        temp = *a;
        *a = *b;
        *b = temp;
    }
}
```

As another example of the use of a reference parameter, we revisit the change analysis problem introduced in Program 2.4. Program 7.7 demonstrates how this program could be rewritten using a function to carry out the repetitive process of working out how many of a given coin are needed in making up the change.

===== **PROGRAM 7.7** =====

This is a rewrite of Program 2.4, the supermarket checkout program that displays the number and denomination of coins required to make up the change from £1 for a purchase costing less than £1 (a whole number of pennies).

```
/* Program 7.7 : Change - Version 2*/

#include <stdio.h>

void HowMany(int CoinValue, int *AmountLeft);

void main (void)
{
    int price, change;

    printf("\nPrice in pence(<100):");
    scanf("%i", &price);
    change = 100 - price;

    printf("Change due is:\n");
    HowMany(50, &change);
    HowMany(20, &change);
    HowMany(10, &change);
    HowMany(5, &change);
    HowMany(2, &change);
    HowMany(1, &change);
    printf("\n");

}

void HowMany(int CoinValue, int *AmountLeft)
{ int coins;
    coins = *AmountLeft/CoinValue;
    *AmountLeft = *AmountLeft % CoinValue;
    printf("%i %is, ", coins, CoinValue);
}
```

The first parameter, CoinValue, passed to the function HowMany is a value parameter indicating the denomination of the coin to be allocated next. The second, *AmountLeft, is a reference parameter that initially contains the amount of change currently remaining to be allocated. The function alters this variable to contain the amount remaining after coins of the specified denomination have been allocated.

7.4 ■ Functions with results

If the result of some process is a single value then a function that returns a value is sometimes an elegant alternative to a void function. We have already seen how to use the standard functions sqrt, sin, cos and so on. C functions that produce results in this way are true functions in the mathematical sense.

First let us look at the ways in which a function differs from a void function. Certainly, they are both separate modules of program text referred to by name, but they differ in the way in which they are called. Functions are called by using them in arithmetic expressions – that is the first difference. The second difference is that the result of obeying the function is a single value that replaces the function call in the originating expression. Let us illustrate this by considering:

```
y = x + sqrt(2);
```

When this statement is being obeyed, the computer obeys the definition of the function sqrt, and a number – the result of obeying the function – replaces the subexpression sqrt(2). In the case of a standard function like sqrt, the definition of the function is already stored as part of the standard library, but it is also possible for you to define your own functions. They are defined in the program just as void functions are defined. A function defined in this way can then be used in exactly the same way as the standard functions.

An example appears in Program 7.8. The effect of calling a function is the calculation of a single result. The result has a type, which must be specified. This is done by writing the name of this type before the function name in the function heading. The C system can use this type information to ensure that the function is used in an appropriate context.

Since calling a function produces a single result, we must indicate, somewhere in the function definition, what this result is to be. In the function definition, we use the keyword return followed by an expression which is to be returned as the value of the subexpression used to call the function.

When Program 7.8 is obeyed, evaluation of the subexpression max(a,b) causes the function definition to be obeyed with first set to the value of a and second set to the value of b. If the function is called when we have the situation:

a 1.5   b 5.64

then the function definition is obeyed with:

first 1.5   second 5.64

and the statement:

```
return second;
```

================= **PROGRAM 7.8** =================

This program reads three pairs of numbers and adds the larger of the first pair, the larger of the second pair and the larger of the third pair.

```
/* Program 7.8 : Add */
#include <stdio.h>
float max(float first, float second);
void main(void)
{ float a, b, p, q, x, y;
    scanf("%f%f%f%f%f%f", &a, &b, &p, &q, &x, &y);
    printf("%f\n", max(a, b) + max(p, q) + max(x, y));
}
float max(float first, float second)
{
    if (first > second)
        return first;
    else
        return second;
}
```

is obeyed as a result of obeying the `if` statement. The value of the subexpression `max(a,b)` will therefore be `5.64`, and this is the value that will be used in subsequent evaluation of the larger expression:

```
max(a,b) + max(p,q) + max(x,y)
```

If the main body of the program had included a statement such as:

```
printf("%f\n", max(63.45, 61.23) );
```

the function would have been obeyed with:

first `63.45`   second `61.23`

and the value returned as the result of the function in this case would be `63.45`, this value being printed by the `printf` statement. The actual parameters can of course be any expressions that will have `float` values when the program is obeyed. This means that the actual parameters in a call of the function can themselves involve further function calls. We have already seen how we can do this with the standard functions:

```
z = sqrt(pow(x, 2) + pow(y, 2));
printf("%f\n", pow(pow(pow(z,2),2),2) );
```

Our function `max` can be used in the same way:

```
printf("%f\n", max(sqrt(2), sqrt(3) ) );
```

will print:

    1.73

and:

    printf("%f\n", max(max(6.2, 7.4), max(2.3, 9.5)));

will print:

    9.5

In the last case, the function calls are evaluated as follows:

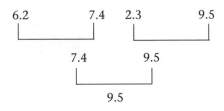

Note that the use of the function name within its own definition has a special meaning which is beyond the scope of this book.

Functions with results can also have reference parameters, but the use of this facility is looked upon as being bad programming practice and we shall avoid it.

SUMMARY OF CHAPTER 7

Key points

- A simple **void function** can be used to emphasize the logical structure of a program.
- A variable declared at the top of the program outside the function definitions is **global** and is accessible from within all of the functions in the program. A variable declared within the body of a function is **local** and is accessible only within the text of that function.
- A void function with one or more **parameters** can be passed information from the point in the program where it is called.
- A **reference parameter** allows the function to change the contents of a variable which is given as a parameter. In the function heading, the name of a reference parameter is preceded by the * character.
- The & character is known as the addressing operator and is used to supply the address of a variable when calling a function with a reference parameter.
- The * character used before a name allows us to access the contents of a reference parameter in the body of a function definition.

- A function that returns a value is a true function in the mathematical sense. For example, an integer function can return an integer value. A call to such a function can be written on the right-hand side of an assignment statement, on its own, or as part of a larger expression.

Good programming practice

- Use global variables as little as possible, if at all. Pass values and variables required by a function as parameters.
- If a program consists of clearly identifiable separate logical units, define each of these units as a separate C function.

Common problems	
Problem	**Symptom**
Variable declared in the wrong place, for example locally instead of globally.	This will result in compiler error messages to the effect that a variable has not been declared. Do *not* simply declare the variable for a second time in a different place – see next problem.
Variable declared in two different places.	Program will have two distinct variables referring to different storage locations. If this was not the intention, then program behaviour will be unpredictable.
Failure to use a reference parameter when appropriate.	The function in question will change a local copy of the parameter concerned and the changes will not be transmitted back to the calling code.
Missing & before a reference parameter in a function call.	Any value placed in the parameter by the function will actually be placed somewhere else in the computer memory – this could destroy the contents of one of your other variables or, more seriously, memory being used by other software on your computer. Program may behave oddly or computer may seize up completely.
Missing * before use of a reference parameter in a function definition.	May cause a compiler error message or may simply produce some warnings and the program will still run, producing unpredictable results.

EXERCISES FOR CHAPTER 7

(1) A company's employees are paid $19.73 per hour for a standard 35-hour week.
Overtime hours during the week are paid at 1.25 times this rate and overtime hours at
the weekend are paid at 1.5 times this rate. Income tax is paid at a rate of 30% on the
first $200 of a week's pay, 40% on the next $300 and 50% on the remainder. Write a
program that accepts, as input, the number of weekday overtime hours worked and
the number of weekend overtime hours worked by an employee in one week. The
program should print a payslip, giving details of the employee's normal pay, overtime
pay and deductions for that week. The main part of your program should include the
three function calls:

```
AddNormalHoursPay();
AddOvertimeHoursPay();
DeductIncomeTax();
```

(2) A bank normally levies charges on a customer's cheque account at the rate of 20p per
debit entry. However, charges are waived if the daily balance never falls below £50
over a 30-day period. A day's transactions on an account are recorded as a list of
positive and negative numbers, where the positive numbers represent payments into
the account and the negative numbers represent a cheque withdrawal charged to the
account. Each negative entry in the list is immediately followed by the four-digit serial
number of the cheque. Such a daily list is terminated by a zero. Thirty such lists
covering a period of 30 consecutive days have been typed one after another into a file
and the amount of the customer's previous balance has been typed at the start of the
file. Write a program that prints the customer's bank statement for the 30-day period.
Use functions to make the logical structure of your program clear.

(3) Rewrite your solution for Exercise 6, Chapter 2 using functions, as illustrated in
Program 7.7.

(4) A motor rally takes place all on one day and, for each car, a start time and a finish time
are recorded. Each car also has a handicap time, which is to be subtracted from the true
time taken for the rally in order to determine an adjusted time. Write a program that
reads the start time, finish time and handicap time for one car and prints the true time
and the adjusted time for that car. Each time is input as two integers (hours and

minutes) separated by a space. The program should do all of its calculations in minutes, the conversion from hours and minutes being done by a function `readtime`, which reads a time in hours and minutes, and the conversion back to hours and minutes being done by a function `writetime`.

(5) Write a program to evaluate the expression:

$$x^5 + y^4 + z^3$$

where *x*, *y* and *z* are supplied as input. Your program should include a function `power` that can be used to raise a floating point number to an integer power. For example, the expression:

```
power(x, 5)
```

would have the value x^5. Do not use the function `pow` from the standard library.

(6) Rewrite your solution to Exercise 7, Chapter 5, using a function that processes the readings from one machine.

(7) Write a function that takes a month number and a year number and returns the number of days in the month. Rewrite your solution to Exercise 8, Chapter 6 using this function.

(8) There should be a library called `graphics.h` in your C system. Facilities provided in this library vary from one C system to another. Look at the documentation for your graphics library – you should find functions for switching to graphics mode, for moving around the screen and for drawing lines on the screen. Write a carefully structured program that will draw a stylized picture of a house, such as that shown in Figure 7.1.

Your program should include functions such as `DrawAHouse`, `DrawAWindow` and `DrawADoor`, which take parameters indicating the position and size of the object to be drawn.

(9) Now extend your program for Exercise 8 to draw a street of houses, all of different shapes. The position and size data for each house in the street could be read from a file.

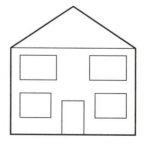

Figure 7.1 A stylized picture of a house drawn by C.

CHAPTER 8

Working with characters

Until now, characters typed as input to our programs have been numeric characters grouped together to represent numbers in the usual way. Many computer applications involve handling non-numeric data. For example, an organization may want to use a computer program to process a list of its customers' names and addresses; a telephone customer account number might be a combination of letters and digits which has to be handled by a computer program; a student of literature might use a computer program to analyse a piece of text under study. C programs usually have to store and process such non-numeric data one character at a time.

8.1 ■ Character variables and character input

In this section we shall introduce some C facilities that will enable us to write programs that manipulate the individual characters supplied as input to a program.

PROGRAM 8.1

This program reads three characters and writes these three characters in reverse order.

```
/* Program 8.1 : Reverse */
#include <stdio.h>
void main(void)
{
   char first, second, third;
   scanf("%c%c%c", &first, &second, &third);
   printf("%c%c%c\n", third, second, first);
}
```

In addition to the types `int` and `float` we now have the type `char`. In Program 8.1, `first`, `second` and `third` are variables in each of which a single character can be stored. If this program is supplied with input:

    bat

then after obeying the `scanf` statement, the character variables contain:

    first ⸢'b'⸥   second ⸢'a'⸥   third ⸢'t'⸥

In C, character values are always written in single quotation marks ('), not to be confused with the double quotation marks (") used for strings. On this occasion, the `printf` statement has the same effect as:

    printf ("%c%c%c\n", 't', 'a', 'b');

and output thus consists of:

    tab

Input of:

    *-+

results in output of:

    +-*

Input of:

    467

results in output of:

    764

In this last case, you should note that, although the three characters in the input could be treated as making up a single number, Program 8.1 reads and stores the input as three separate digits, each being stored in a separate character variable.

Frequently a program for manipulating characters has to distinguish one group of characters from another. For example, a program manipulating the words in a piece of text may have to treat the punctuation characters between words differently from the letters constituting the words. In other cases, a program may be required to distinguish separate lines of input. Program 8.2 illustrates this by ignoring any spaces that appear at the start of the input.

Note that instead of the statement:

    scanf("%c", &first);

we can use:

    first = getchar();

where `getchar` is a standard function from `stdio` that returns the next character from the input.

Given input of:

    cat

━━━━━━━━━━━━━ **PROGRAM 8.2** ━━━━━━━━━━━━━

This program ignores any spaces that may be typed at the start of the input, and then prints all permutations of the three characters that follow.

```c
/* Program 8.2 : Anagrams */
#include <stdio.h>
void main(void)
{
   char first, second, third;
   do {
      first = getchar();
   } while (first == ' ');
   second = getchar(); third = getchar();
   printf("%c%c%c  ", first, second, third);
   printf("%c%c%c\n", first, third, second);
   printf("%c%c%c  ", second, first, third);
   printf("%c%c%c\n", second, third, first);
   printf("%c%c%c  ", third, first, second);
   printf("%c%c%c\n", third, second, first);
}
```

(preceded by any number of spaces), Program 8.2 produces output:

```
cat  cta
act  atc
tca  tac
```

When input for a program is being typed at a keyboard, a special end-of-line key is pressed to mark the end of a line. Usually this will be the RETURN or ENTER key. Pressing this key inserts a special 'end-of-line' character in the input which, when written in a program, appears as '\n'. Although it takes an extra keystroke to type, '\n' is treated as a single character just like 'z' or '+'. We have already used \n in printf statements to start a new line. Thus a program can count how many characters were typed before the end-of-line key was pressed:

```c
char NextChar; int count;
      .
      .
      .
   count = 0;
   NextChar = getchar();
   while (NextChar != '\n')
   {
      count++;
      NextChar = getchar();
   }
```

Here, we have used a `while` loop in case the input line happens to be blank.

When a character variable containing '\n' is output using `printf`, a new line will be started. Consider the following program fragment:

```
char ch1, ch2, ch3, ch4;
        .
        .
        .
ch1 = getchar(); ch2 = getchar();
ch3 = getchar(); ch4 = getchar();
printf("%c%c%c%c", ch1, ch2, ch3, ch4);
```

If we supply input:

```
abcd
```

the `printf` statement will print:

```
abcd
```

Given input of:

```
ab
c
```

where the end-of-line key is pressed immediately after the 'b', output will be

```
ab
c
```

Finally, do not confuse the notions of a character and the name of a variable. Consider:

```
char a;
        .
        .
        .
a = getchar();
printf("%c%c\n", a, 'a');
```

The `printf` statement will print the contents of the variable called a followed by the character 'a'.

Input	Output
z	za
*	*a
a	aa

8.2 ■ Characters as function parameters

Program 8.3 illustrates how a character can be passed as a parameter to a function.

The function `PrintChars` is defined in terms of two parameters, ch and n. When this function is called, the character supplied as its first parameter is printed a number

PROGRAM 8.3

This is a variation on Program 6.6.

```c
/* Program 8.3 : Framed Triangle 2 */

#include <stdio.h>
void PrintRow(int row, int rows);
void PrintChars(char ch, int n);

void main(void)
{
   int rows, WidthOfPicture, NextRow;
   printf("\nheight of triangle:"); scanf("%i", &rows);
   WidthOfPicture = 2*rows + 1;

   PrintChars('.',WidthOfPicture);
   printf("\n");

   for(NextRow=1; NextRow<=rows; NextRow++)
      PrintRow(NextRow, rows);

   PrintChars('.',WidthOfPicture);
   printf("\n");

}

void PrintRow(int row, int rows)
{
   PrintChars('.', rows + 1 - row);
   PrintChars('*', 2*row - 1);
   PrintChars('.', rows + 1 - row);
   printf("\n");
}

void PrintChars(char ch,  int n)
{
   int count;
   for (count = 1; count <= n; count++) putchar(ch);
}
```

of times which is specified as a value for the second parameter. (putchar simply displays a character on the screen.) For example, if we call the function as follows:

```c
PrintChars('*', 5);
```

ch is given the value '*', n is given the value 5 and the function definition is obeyed. Output is therefore:

```
*****
```

The actual parameters supplied to this function can in fact be any two expressions, provided that the first represents a character and the second represents an integer.

For example, if `symbol` is a character variable and `number` is an integer variable, then the fragment:

```
symbol = 'a';   number = 5;
PrintChars(symbol,number);
PrintChars('x', 2*number + 1);
```

will output:

```
aaaaaxxxxxxxxxxx
```

8.3 ▪ Reading character data from files

As we saw in Chapter 5, a program can read its data from a file as well as from the keyboard. Whenever an attempt to read beyond the last character in a file has been made, this can be detected using the `feof` function. For example, the following fragment of program will count how many characters (including end-of-line markers) there are in a given input file:

```
FILE *text;
text = fopen("TEXT.DAT","r");
count = 0;
NextChar = getc(text);
while (!feof(text))
{
   count++;
   NextChar = getc(text);
}
fclose(text);
printf("There are %i characters in the file", count);
```

Note the use of the function `getc` to read a character from a given text file, as opposed to `getchar`, which reads from the keyboard. Program 8.4 elaborates on the above theme by counting the number of occurrences of the letter 'e' in the file.

8.4 ▪ Character ordering

When we are handling numbers, we can ask if one number comes before or after another number by using expressions such as x < y, count >= 3, r <= 23.47, and so on. We are able to do this because there is a natural ordering defined for the integers and floating point numbers. In fact, there is also an ordering defined for the characters that can be handled by a C program. Characters can be compared using the operators <, >, <= and >=. You will find in particular that:

PROGRAM 8.4

This program counts the number of occurrences of a given character in a piece of text supplied in an input file. The given character is specified as a named constant.

```c
/* Program 8.4 : Character count */

#include <stdio.h>
#define GIVENCH 'e'

void main(void)
{
    int occurrences; char nextch;
    FILE *text;
    text = fopen("TEXT.DAT","r");

    occurrences = 0;

    nextch = getc(text);
    while (!feof(text))
    {
        if (nextch == GIVENCH) occurrences++;
        nextch = getc(text);
    }

    fclose(text);

    printf("The character %c", GIVENCH);
    printf(" appears %i times.\n", occurrences);

}
```

'A' is before 'B' with no other character in between.
'B' is before 'C' with no other character in between.
'C' is before 'D' with no other character in between.
.
.
.
'Y' is before 'Z' with no other character in between.

'a' is before 'b' with no other character in between.
'b' is before 'c' with no other character in between.
'c' is before 'd' with no other character in between.
.
.
.
'y' is before 'z' with no other character in between.

and

'0' is before '1' with no other character in between.
'1' is before '2' with no other character in between.
.
.
.
'8' is before '9' with no other character in between.

We can therefore test whether the character in the variable ch is alphabetic by using:

```
if ( ((ch >= 'A') && (ch <= 'Z')) || ((ch >= 'a') && (ch <= 'z')) ) ...
```

However, there is a predefined function, isalpha() in ctype.h that achieves this:

```
if (isalpha(ch)) ...
```

Similarly, we could test whether a character is a numeric digit by using:

```
if ((ch >= '0') && (ch <= '9')) ...
```

or by using the predefined function isdigit():

```
if (isdigit(ch)) ...
```

In general, we shall probably not be interested in whether a character such as '*' comes before or after a character such as '='. In fact, the position of such non-alphanumeric characters in the ordering may vary from one system to another.
   Programs 8.5, 8.6 and 8.7 illustrate the use of these features.

=== PROGRAM 8.5 ===

This reads one character and prints a message indicating whether it is alphabetic, numeric or otherwise.

```
/* Program 8.5 : Classify Character */
#include <stdio.h>
#include <ctype.h>
void main(void)
{
  char character;
  printf("Type character for analysis:");
  character = getchar();
  if (isalpha(character))
    printf("That character is alphabetic.\n");
  else
    if (isdigit(character))
      printf("That character is numeric.\n");
    else
      printf("That character is not alphanumeric.\n");
}
```

═══════════════════ **PROGRAM 8.6** ═══════════════════

This program reads a word and counts how many letters it contains. Any non-alphabetic characters before the word are ignored and the last letter of the word is followed in the input by a non-alphabetic character.

```
/* Program 8.6 : Word Length */

#include <stdio.h>
#include <ctype.h>

void main(void)
{
   char NextChar; int LetterCount;

   do {
      NextChar = getchar();
   } while (!isalpha(NextChar));

   /* At this point, NextChar will contain */
   /* the first letter of the word.        */

   LetterCount = 0;
   do {
      LetterCount++;
      NextChar = getchar();
   } while (isalpha(NextChar));

   /* At this point, NextChar will contain */
   /* the first character after the word.  */

   printf("No. of letters: %i\n", LetterCount);

}
```

Program 8.8 illustrates how a piece of text can be processed on a word-by-word basis. It counts the total number of words in a sentence and counts the number of four-letter words in the same sentence. We assume for simplicity that the sentence is terminated by a full stop typed immediately after the last word. We can summarize what we want this program to do as follows:

```
words = 0; fourwords = 0;
do
{
```
   Find start of next word.
   Read next word and count letters in it.
```
   words++;
   if (letters == 4) fourwords++;
} while (nextch != '.');
```

━━━━━━━━━━━━━━━━━━━━ **PROGRAM 8.7** ━━━━━━━━━━━━━━━━━━━━

Given a piece of text, this program counts the percentage of the letters in the text that are equal to a given letter.

```
/* Program 8.7 : Letter Frequency */
#include <stdio.h>
#include <ctype.h>
#define GIVEN_LETTER 'e'

void main(void)
{
  int LetterCount, GivenLetterCount;
  char character;
  FILE *text;
  text = fopen("TEXT.DAT","r");

  LetterCount = 0; GivenLetterCount = 0;
  character = getc(text);
  while (!feof(text))
  {
    if (isalpha(character))
    {
      LetterCount++;
      if (character == GIVEN_LETTER)
        GivenLetterCount++;
    }
    character = getc(text);
  }

  fclose(text);

  printf("%f per cent of the letters were %c.\n",
            100.0 * GivenLetterCount/LetterCount, GIVEN_LETTER);

}
```

Finding the start of a word and then counting the letters in the word involves obeying two separate loops, one after the other, as in Program 8.6, but in this case the section of program containing these loops must be obeyed once for each word in the sentence as outlined above. Instead of writing these loops out explicitly inside the word loop, we shall use functions for these two subsidiary operations, the loops being contained inside the functions. Thus, the structure of the program will reflect the way it was designed. We shall arrange that after the start of a word has been

========= **PROGRAM 8.8** =========

This program counts the total number of words in a sentence and counts the number of four-letter words in the same sentence.

```c
/* Program 8.8 : Count Four-Letter Words */

#include <stdio.h>
#include <ctype.h>

void FindStartOfWord(void);
int LettersInWord(void);

char nextch;

void main(void)
{
   int letters, words, fourwords;
   words = 0; fourwords = 0;
   do
   {
     FindStartOfWord();
     letters = LettersInWord();
     words++;
     if (letters == 4) fourwords++;
   } while (nextch != '.');

   printf("Words in sentence: %i\n", words);
   printf("4-letter words: %i\n", fourwords);
}

void FindStartOfWord(void)
{
   do
   {
     nextch = getchar();
   } while (!isalpha(nextch));
}

int LettersInWord(void)
{
   int count;
   count = 0;
   do
   {
     count++;
     nextch = getchar();
   } while (isalpha(nextch));

   return count;
}
```

found, the variable nextch contains the first character of the word and, after a word has been read, nextch contains the first character after the word. The complete program is presented as Program 8.8. Because the variable nextch is referred to in all three functions, it has to be declared globally. We could have avoided this by passing it as a reference parameter to each of the subsidiary functions in which it is being updated, but this seems rather excessive.

8.5 ■ Further facilities for character manipulation

The ordering of characters introduced in the previous section is not the only feature shared with integers. In fact, char variables are very similar to int variables in terms of the ways in which they can be manipulated by the programmer. For example, to find the 'predecessor' of a given character, we can subtract one from its value:

```
printf("%c %c\n", 'b'-1, 'b');
```

will print:

```
ab
```

Similarily, we can add one to obtain the 'successor' of a given character:

```
ch = 'j';
printf("%c%c%c\n", ch-1, ch, ch+1);
```

will print:

```
ijk
```

We use this in Program 8.9, but we need to be careful not to overshoot the end of the alphabet if we want the result to be another letter.

Because of the ordering defined for the characters, we can use a character variable as the control variable in a for loop:

```
char letter;

for (letter = 'a'; letter <= 'z'; letter++)
   putchar(letter);
printf("\n");
```

will print:

```
abcdefghijklmnopqrstuvwxyz
```

The statement:

```
for (letter = 'z'; letter >= 'a'; letter--)
   putchar(letter);
```

will print:

```
zyxwvutsrqponmlkjihgfedcba
```

═══════ **PROGRAM 8.9** ═══════

A message is to be coded by replacing each letter in the message by the succeeding letter in the alphabet, 'z' being replaced by 'a'. This program reads a piece of text from a file and prints the message in its coded form. The line by line structure of the original message is maintained, since end-of-line markers are copied unchanged along with any other non-alphabetic characters.

```c
/* Program 8.9 : Code */

#include <stdio.h>
#include <ctype.h>

char coded(char ch);

void main(void)
{
   char character;
   FILE *text;
   text = fopen("TEXT.DAT","r");

   character = getc(text);
   while (!feof(text))
   {
      putchar(coded(character));
      character = getc(text);
   }

   fclose(text);
}

char coded(char ch)
{
    if (isalpha(ch))
       if (ch == 'z')
          return 'a';
       else
          return ch+1;
    else
       return ch;
}
```

Each character has an 'ordinal number' (an integer) associated with it. A character's ordinal number is determined by the position of the character in the overall character ordering. In fact, it is possible to display the contents of a char variable using %i for the format code in a printf statement. The output will be the integer which corresponds to the character that the variable contains. The converse is also true – a suitable int variable can be displayed using %c. This will print the character corresponding to the numeric value in the variable. For example, you could find out what characters correspond to numbers 0 to 63 by obeying:

```
for (i = 0; i <= 63; i++)
   printf("%i %c ", i, i);
printf("\n");
```

The ordinal numbers associated with the lower-case alphabetic characters could be printed by using:

```
for (ch = 'a'; ch <= 'z'; ch++)
   printf("%c %i ", ch, ch);
printf("\n");
```

In general, you do not need to know what the ordinal numbers are, so long as you remember that, for example, the alphabetic characters have consecutive ordinal numbers. We could print the *n*th letter of the alphabet by using:

```
scanf("%i", &n);
printf("%c\n", 'a'+n-1);
```

In Program 8.10, values greater than one can be 'added' to letters to implement a more elaborate code than that in Program 8.9. We again have to deal with the possibility of the addition taking us off the end of the alphabet.

Finally, we present a facility that enables a program to 'give back' a character it has taken from the input. This is useful when we wish to look at the next character before deciding what to do with it. For example, we may discover that the character we read is the first digit of an integer. Unless we put back the character after we have looked at it, the integer that we subsequently read using scanf will have its first digit missing. The standard function we are going to use is:

```
ungetc(c, filevar);
```

which gives back the character c to the file whose variable appears as the second parameter. We can even 'give back' a character to the keyboard by:

```
ungetc(c, stdin);
```

where stdin stands for 'standard input'. The circumstances in which this might be used are illustrated in Program 8.11.

======= **PROGRAM 8.10** =======

This program codes a message with a slightly different cipher from that used in Program 8.9. In this case, each letter in the message is replaced by the letter a given number of places ahead in the alphabet. This given number is defined as a named constant. As before, the alphabet is treated as circular, 'a' being assumed to follow 'z'.

```c
/* Program 8.10 : Code Shift */

#include <stdio.h>
#include <ctype.h>
#define SHIFT 5

char coded(char ch);

void main(void)
{
   char character; int ordinal;
   FILE *text;
   text = fopen("TEXT.DAT","r");

   character = getc(text);
   while (!feof(text))
   {
      putchar(coded(character));
      character = getc(text);
   }

   fclose(text);
}

char coded(char ch)
{ char newch;
   if (isalpha(ch))
   {
      newch = ch + SHIFT;
      if (newch > 'z') newch -= 26;
   }
   else newch = ch;
   return newch;
}
```

================ **PROGRAM 8.11** ================

This program reads an integer that tells it how many further integers are to be read and added together. The integers in the input may be interspersed with extraneous text that must be ignored by the program. There will be a question mark at the end of the text to be processed.

```c
/* Program 8.11 : Add Up */

#include <stdio.h>
#include <ctype.h>

void main(void)
{
   int HowMany, count, next, total;
   char c;

   /* 'First' section */
   do
      c = getchar();
   while (!isdigit(c));
   ungetc(c, stdin);
   scanf("%i", &HowMany);

   /* 'Second' section */
   total = 0;
   for (count = 1; count <= HowMany; count++)
   {
      do
        c = getchar();
      while (!isdigit(c));
      ungetc(c, stdin);
      scanf("%i", &next);
      total += next;
   }

   /* 'Third' section */
   do c = getchar(); while (c != '?');
   printf("Total is: %i\n", total);
}
```

Given the following input:

```
On our street there are 4 types of restaurant:
There are 13 Indian, 21 Italian,
4 Balti and 16 Chinese.
How many restaurants are there?
```

Program 8.11 outputs:

```
Total is 54
```

The section of the program labelled 'first' finds and reads the first integer in the data. When the `scanf` statement is obeyed, the first digit of the integer has been put back on the input, and is available to be processed by the `scanf` statement. The section of the program marked 'third' does not serve any useful purpose as the program stands. However, we might later want to extend the program to deal with further input of some sort. This section of the program simply ensures that the program reads all characters associated with the data that has been processed so far.

In summary, the keyboard is currently one of our main channels of communication with the computer. For this reason, there are many important application areas for the techniques that have been introduced in this chapter.

SUMMARY OF CHAPTER 8

Key points

- Character variables are used in situations where we need to process text.
- Instead of using `scanf`, we can use `getchar` to read a single character from the user at the keyboard.
- The return/enter key causes the special character `'\n'` to appear in the input.
- We use `getc` to read a single character from a file.
- Characters can be compared using the relational operators.
- We can test whether a character is alphabetic or numeric by using `isalpha` and `isdigit`, respectively.
- Characters exhibit some integer-like behaviour; for example, it is possible to add to or subtract from a character variable.

Common problems	
Problem	**Symptom**
Getting out of step with the data – every key-press counts as a character, and forgetting to ignore spaces or end-of-line characters is common.	Program will process the wrong character in the wrong place. For example, it may print out blank lines that were not intended if the end-of-line character is printed by mistake.
Failure to test correctly for the end-of-file marker – remember that `feof` is not `TRUE` until an attempt is made to read beyond the end of a file.	The program will attempt to process characters beyond the end of the file.

Debugging **tip**

■ Print each important character as it is processed to see if the program is progressing correctly through the data.

━━━━━━━━━━━━━━━ EXERCISES FOR CHAPTER 8 ━━━━━━━━━━━━━━━

(1) Write a program that will read a word of four letters. The word is to be printed again by the program, except that if it is the same as a given word (specified by means of four named character constants), it should be censored, the middle two characters being replaced by asterisks.

(2) Write a program that will read a file of text and that will print a message indicating the total number of alphabetic characters in the text and another message indicating the total number of non-alphabetic characters (including end-of-line markers).

(3) The input file for a program consists of a list of names, one name to a line. Each name consists of two forenames followed by a surname. The two forenames and the surname are separated from each other by one space; for example:

```
James Jardine McGregor
Richard James McGregor
John Stuart Smith
Alan Henry Watt
        .
        .
        .
```

Write a program that reads such a file and prints each name in the form of a surname followed by two initials; for example:

```
McGregor, J.J.
McGregor, R.J.
Smith, J.S.
Watt, A.H.
      .
      .
      .
```

(4) Each line in a file contains a distance in miles (an integer) followed by the name of a town which lies at that distance from London. Write a program that will read this file and print a list of the names of towns that are less than 100 miles from London.

(5) A message is decoded by replacing each letter in the message by the letter *n* steps behind in the alphabet. The alphabet is considered to be circular and 'z' is treated as being one step behind 'a'. Write a program that will print a table for use in the manual coding and decoding of messages for a given value of *n*. For example, with *n* = 4, the table would be:

```
coded letter:     abcdefghijklmnopqrstuvwxyz
decoded letter:   wxyzabcdefghijklmnopqrstuv
```

(6) A file contains information about a company's salaried employees. Each line of the file contains the name of an employee (made up to exactly 25 characters by inserting extra spaces if necessary), followed by the annual salary in pounds. Write a program that will print a monthly payslip for each employee in the file. Assume that tax is deducted at a flat rate of 30%.

(7) Write a program that counts how many words there are in a sentence and also counts how many of these words begin with the letter 'a'. The last word in the sentence is followed immediately by a full stop.

(8) A music shop has done a stocktaking of all the musical instruments in stock. The list is to be input to a computer program in the form, for example:

```
102 violins, 24 cellos.
1 french horn, 23 trumpets and 3 cornets;
.
.
.
etc.
```

where the punctuation is arbitrary. Assume that each instrument is mentioned only once in the list. Write a program that ignores the non-numeric characters and reports the number of different instruments in stock (the number of numerical entries in the file) as well as the total number of instruments in stock.

(9) Write a program that reads a piece of text and checks that it obeys the spelling rule: 'i' comes before 'e' except after 'c'.

(10) A piece of text has been typed into a file with little attention being paid to the spacing between words or to the line-by-line layout of the text. (For the purposes of this example, a 'word' is any group of non-space characters.) The last word in the text is terminated by the character '*'. Write a program that reads the text and prints it with an improved layout as follows:

(a) There should be no spaces at the start of a line and there should never be more than one space between words on a line.

(b) A new line should be started immediately after printing a word if more than 50 characters have already been printed on the current line.

The main part of your program should be:

```
while (NextChar != '*')
{
    processsspaces();
    copyaword();
}
```

(11) A legal document contains a number of sentences and it has been typed into a file
with little attention being paid to its layout. The last word in each sentence is terminated by a full stop and the last full stop is followed immediately by the character '*'.
The document is to be printed with the sentences numbered 1, 2, 3..., each sentence
starting on a new line. The output document should otherwise satisfy the layout
requirements specified in the previous exercise. Write a program to do this.

CHAPTER 9

Collections of values: Arrays

If a program systematically processes a collection of variables, it may not be convenient for the programmer to give each of these variables a different name. For example, it would be rather tedious to write:

```
TotalPrice = PriceOfHammer + PriceOfSaw   +
             PriceOfAxe    + PriceOfPlane +
             PriceOfChisel + PriceOfVice  +
             PriceOfScrewd + PriceOfSpanner;
```

Instead of giving such a group of variables separate names, it is often more convenient to give them a collective name and to refer to the individual variables in the collection by subscripts, where the subscripts are numbers.

9.1 ■ One-dimensional arrays

A one-dimensional array is a set of storage locations or variables all of the same type that share the same name, but have different subscripts. For example, the separate variables:

PriceOfHammer	5.77
PriceOfSaw	3.15
PriceOfAxe	2.50
PriceOfPlane	16.33
PriceOfChisel	2.50
PriceOfVice	13.45
PriceOfScrewd	0.86
PriceOfSpanner	1.98

could be stored in a one-dimensional array, which can be visualized as:

PriceOf

PriceOf [0]	5.77
PriceOf [1]	3.15
PriceOf [2]	2.50
PriceOf [3]	16.33
PriceOf [4]	2.50
PriceOf [5]	13.45
PriceOf [6]	0.86
PriceOf [7]	1.98

The numbers in square brackets are the distinguishing subscripts. Arrays have to be declared, and for our example the declaration could be:

```
float PriceOf[8];
```

In this declaration, `PriceOf` is the name of the array. The number in square brackets is the size of the array. It is important to realize that the subscripts for this array run from 0 to 7, and *not* from 1 to 8. In this case there will be no array location whose subscript is 8. This is often a source of confusion for beginners and experts alike. In this example, each item in the array is of type `float`. In a program, the subscript used to select a location of the above array can be an integer constant, an integer variable, or indeed any integer expression, as long as the value of the subscript is in the range 0–7. This has the advantage that we can use a loop to process systematically all of the values in the array (a point discussed in detail in the next section). For example:

```
for (ItemNo = 0; ItemNo <= 7; ItemNo++)
    TotalPrice += PriceOf[ItemNo];
```

Array locations can be manipulated just like simple variables. For example:

```
scanf("%f%f", &PriceOf[0], &PriceOf[1]);
scanf("%f%f", &PriceOf[2], &PriceOf[3]);
scanf("%f%f", &PriceOf[4], &PriceOf[5]);
scanf("%f%f", &PriceOf[6], &PriceOf[7]);

printf("The price of item 0 is %.2f\n", PriceOf[0]);
printf("The price of item 3 is %.2f\n", PriceOf[3]);

printf("The price difference between ");
printf("items 1 and 2 is %.2f\n", fabs(PriceOf[1] - PriceOf[2]));

difference = PriceOf[1] - PriceOf[2];
if (difference > 0)
    printf("Item 1 costs %.2f more than item 2.\n", difference);
else if (difference < 0)
    printf("Item 2 costs %.2f more than item 1.\n", -difference);
```

9.2 ■ Sequential access to one-dimensional arrays

We shall return to the price list example shortly. In Program 9.1, we have declared an array of ten integer locations all named number.

═══════ **PROGRAM 9.1** ═══════

This program reads ten integers and prints them in reverse order.

```
/* Program 9.1 : Reverse */

#include <stdio.h>

void main(void)
{
    int number[10];
    int position;

    for (position = 0; position <= 9; position++)
        scanf("%i", &(number[position]));
    for (position = 9; position >= 0; position--)
        printf("%i\n", number[position]);
}
```

In Program 9.1 the array locations are accessed systematically one after another. This is a very simple example of sequential access. The program reads input integers into successive locations. It then starts at the tenth location (location number 9) and fetches the integers in reverse order, printing them as it goes. A control structure appropriate for these actions is a for statement, and we use the control variable position as an array subscript. The execution of the first for statement proceeds as follows:

Value of 'position'	Statement obeyed
0	scanf("%i", &(number[0]))
1	scanf("%i", &(number[1]))
2	scanf("%i", &(number[2]))
⋮	

It is important to note that each array location has two quantities associated with it:

■ the subscript
■ the contents of the location

There is no reason why all the locations in an array should be used by a program. For example, Program 9.1 could have been made to process a list of varying length by reading the length of the list prior to reading the list itself:

```
int position, ListLength;
scanf("%i", &ListLength);
for (position = 0; position < ListLength; position++)
   scanf("%i", &(number[position]));
for (position = ListLength-1; position >= 0; position--)
   printf("%i\n", number[position]);
```

The program could now process a list of up to ten numbers, provided that the number of values is indicated at the start of the data. For example, to process six numbers, the user could type:

```
6    11 23 33 45 58 64
```

and only locations 0 to 5 of the array would be used. Locations 6 to 9 would remain undefined, which is no problem as long as the program does not subsequently try to use values from these locations.

It will frequently be convenient not to use location 0 of an array if our data is most naturally labelled from 1 upwards. C programmers are often reluctant to do this, but we feel that a closer match between the structure of the data in the program and the problem being represented results in less likelihood of errors. The following has exactly the same effect as Program 9.1, but the values processed are numbered from 1 to 10, rather than from 0 to 9. Notice that the array is now of size 11, but location 0 is not used:

```
int number[11];
int position;

for (position = 1; position <= 10; position++)
   scanf("%i", &(number[position]));
for (position = 10; position >= 1; position--)
   printf("%i\n", number[position]);
```

Another example of sequential access appears in Program 9.2, which uses the simple price list introduced earlier.

We can initialize the contents of an array when it is declared, and we have done this to the PriceOf table in Program 9.2 by listing the initial values in braces. This simulates a more realistic situation, where the table would be initialized by reading prices from a file.

The next two programs are very similar to each other, except that one *does not* need an array and one *does*. Program 9.3 does not use an array – there is no need to store any of the data for subsequent reference. It is a common error among new programmers to use arrays unnecessarily. Program 9.4, a simple elaboration of Program 9.3, does require an array. When you have studied these programs, you should compare them carefully and make sure you appreciate why arrays are needed in some cases and not in others.

═══════════════ **PROGRAM 9.2** ═══════════════

Given a price list containing four prices, and a list of four numbers indicating the quantity purchased of each of the four items, this program calculates the total price.

```c
/* Program 9.2 : Prices */

#include <stdio.h>

void main(void)
{
   int ItemNo, quantity;
   float total;
   float PriceOf[4] = { 5.77, 3.15, 2.50, 1.35 };

   total = 0;
   for (ItemNo = 0; ItemNo <= 3; ItemNo++)
   {
      scanf("%i", &quantity);
      total += quantity*PriceOf[ItemNo];
   }

   printf("The total cost is %.2f.\n", total);
}
```

Program 9.3 does a daily sales analysis for a department store and produces a simple histogram, of which the following is an example:

```
         Total sales for each dept.(in 10s)
         ----------------------------------
         1 *************
         2 ***********************************
         3 ************************
dept. no. 4 ********************************
         5 *********
         6 ********
         7 *********************************************
         8 *****
```

The *length* of each line indicates visually the total sales in each of eight departments, and is easier and quicker to interpret than a list of eight numbers. The total sales for each department is approximately indicated by the number of stars on each line multiplied by 10. We are constraining the histogram to a reasonable width by representing each department's sales in tens. Program 9.3 illustrates the basic techniques used in drawing such diagrams.

━━━━━ **PROGRAM 9.3** ━━━━━

This program prints a histogram, given a file containing a list of eight numbers representing the daily sales total for each of eight departments. (We assume that dividing each number by 10 gives a display of suitable width.)

```
/* Program 9.3 : Histogram */

#include <stdio.h>

void main(void)
{
    int dept, col, DeptSales, SalesIn10s;
    FILE *sales;

    sales = fopen("SALES.DAT", "r");

    printf("            Total sales for each dept. (in 10s)\n");
    printf("            -----------------------------------\n");
    for (dept = 1; dept <= 8; dept++)
    {
        if (dept == 4) printf("dept. no. 4 ");
        else printf("%11i ", dept);
        fscanf(sales, "%i", &DeptSales);
        SalesIn10s = DeptSales  / 10;
        for (col = 1; col =< SalesIn10s; col++)
            printf("*");
        printf("\n");
    }
    fclose(sales);
}
```

In Program 9.3, we used a *scaling factor* of 10 in order to ensure that the histogram was not too wide. Each departmental total was divided by 10 before plotting. In Program 9.4, we calculate a scaling factor that depends on the maximum value in the data. This requires a preliminary scan through the data to determine this maximum value. The maximum value is then divided by the maximum number of stars that can be plotted across the screen to give a suitable scaling factor. The scaling factor is truncated to a whole number, because whole number multiples will be easier for the user to visualize, and 1 has to be added to it to make quite sure that the stars do not fall off the end of the line.

PROGRAM 9.4

This is the same as Program 9.3 except that this program is to determine a suitable scaling factor. We assume a line width of 60 and that the maximum sales total is much greater than this.

```c
/* Program 9.4 : Histogram 2 */

#include <stdio.h>
#define LINELENGTH 60

void main(void)
{
   int SalesFor[9];
   int dept, col, MaxSoFar, scaling, ScaledTotal;
   FILE *sales;

   sales = fopen("SALES.DAT", "r");

   MaxSoFar = 0;
   for (dept = 1; dept <= 8; dept++)
   {
      fscanf(sales, "%i", &(SalesFor[dept]) );
      if (SalesFor[dept] > MaxSoFar)
         MaxSoFar = SalesFor[dept];
   }
   fclose(sales);

   scaling = 1 + MaxSoFar / LINELENGTH;

   printf("            Total sales for each dept. (in %is)\n", scaling);
   printf("            ------------------------------------\n");
   for (dept = 1; dept <= 8; dept++)
   {
      if (dept == 4) printf("dept. no. 4 ");
      else printf("%11i ",  dept);
      ScaledTotal = SalesFor [dept] / scaling;
      for (col = 1; col <= ScaledTotal; col++)
         printf("*");
      printf("\n");
   }
}
```

9.3 ■ Arrays of characters: Strings

In Program 9.1 we used an array of integers and in Program 9.2 an array of floating point numbers. Program 9.5 uses an array of characters.

════════════════════════ **PROGRAM 9.5** ════════════════════════

This program reads a word, counts the letters in it, and prints the word backwards.

```c
/* Program 9.5 : Word */

#include <stdio.h>

void main(void)
{
  char letter[20];
  char ch;
  int index, i;

  printf("Type a word followed by ENTER\n");
  index = 0;
  ch = getchar();
  while (ch!='\n')
  { letter[index] = ch;
    index += 1;
    ch = getchar();
  }

  printf("The word backwards is:\n");
  for (i = index-1; i >= 0; i--)
    putchar(letter[i]);
  printf("\n");
}
```

The variable `index` in Program 9.5 is used to count the characters in the word and keep track of the next available location in the array of characters being used to store the word. Although this array contains several letters, we have called the array `letter`. This name makes more sense when used in the body of the program, where the name of the array is always used to refer to a single letter of the word.

Arrays of characters are used frequently in programming for storing words, names, addresses and so on. For this reason, C provides a set of special features that make handling arrays of characters much easier. An array of characters is usually referred to as a **string**, and Program 9.6 illustrates how we can achieve the same effect as in Program 9.5 by using string operations.

================= **PROGRAM 9.6** =================

This program reads a word and prints it backwards.

```
/* Program 9.6 : Word 2 */

#include <stdio.h>
#include <string.h>

void main(void)
{
    char word[21];
    int i;

    printf("Type a word followed by ENTER\n");
    scanf("%s",word);

    printf("The word backwards is:\n");
    for (i = strlen(word)-1; i >= 0; i--)
        putchar(word[i]);
    printf("\n");
}
```

In Program 9.6, we have used a new formatting code, %s. This indicates that a sequence of characters is to be read and stored in an array of characters (a string) until a space or end-of-line is encountered. The space or end-of-line is not treated as part of the string. However, a special symbol is stored in the array after the last character of the string to mark the end of the string, and space must be allowed for this when declaring the array.

Note that there is no & symbol before the name of the array that is being given as a parameter to scanf. Array parameters are automatically passed to functions as addresses, and the addressing operator must not be used – even when the function is changing the contents of the array.

A set of string processing functions is provided in the standard library, and in order to use these, we must include a reference to the header file string.h. In Program 9.6 we have used the function strlen, which counts the number of characters in a string.

A useful alternative to using scanf with %s is to use the gets function from stdio.h. When scanf is used, it is assumed that a string being read terminates at the first space or new-line character encountered, whereas gets reads all characters on the line, including spaces. For example, in Program 9.6 we could have replaced:

```
scanf("%s",word);
```

with:

```
gets(word);
```

9.4 ■ Subscript range errors

When an array location is referred to in a program, the value of the subscript must always be within the subscript range that has been declared. Let us consider what would have happened in Program 9.2 if we had typed:

```
for (ItemNo = 0; ItemNo <= 4; ItemNo++)
```

At one stage, the program would attempt to refer to PriceOf[4], which does not exist, and an unpredictable value would be retrieved from a computer memory location that is not part of the array:

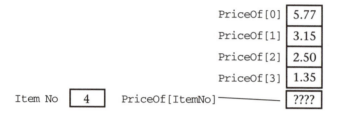

If the program is required to store five prices, the array should be declared as:

```
float PriceOf[5];
```

Now look again at Program 9.5. Here the value of index is used to count and store the characters in the word. If we type more than 20 letters then the program will attempt to store something in letter[20]. This will have the effect of overwriting part of the computer memory that is not part of the array. Subsequent behaviour of a program that does this will be completely unpredictable. We could guard against this eventuality by checking the input data, as suggested in Chapter 6, Section 6.4.

The same problem can arise in a slightly more insidious way in Program 9.6. Here the loop that reads the letters of a word is hidden in the operation of scanf with the %s input code. However, the limits on the array size are still the same, and scanf does not check that the string will fit in the array. If the word is too big, parts of the computer memory outside the array will still be overwritten.

9.5 ■ Random access to one-dimensional arrays

Program 9.7 illustrates the use of an array where the locations are being accessed randomly rather than in a sequential manner.

In Program 9.7 the two locations are not accessed in any particular order. When the program is executed, we could type 3 followed by 1. The program would then access PriceOf[3] followed by PriceOf[1]. We say that the array has been accessed randomly. The process can be illustrated diagramatically as:

====== **PROGRAM 9.7** ======

Given two item numbers in the range 0–3, this program prints the corresponding prices.

```
/* Program 9.7 : Prices 2 */
#include <stdio.h>
void main(void)
{
   float PriceOf[4] = {5.77, 3.15, 2.50, 1.35};
   int itema, itemb;

   scanf("%i %i", &itema, &itemb);
   printf("Item no. %i costs %.2f.\n", itema, PriceOf[itema]);
   printf("Item no. %i costs %.2f.\n", itemb, PriceOf[itemb]);

}
```

The two numbers typed from the keyboard are placed in the integer variables itema and itemb. The contents of itema are used to select one of the four locations of PriceOf. The process is then repeated for itemb. In this case, output would be:

```
item no. 3 costs 1.35
item no. 1 costs 3.15
```

If a number other than 0, 1, 2 or 3 had been typed as input, the program would have produced nonsense.

The next three programs use a mixture of sequential and random access.

In Program 9.8, the array VotesFor is used to accumulate the vote counts for each candidate. Note that there are seven locations in this array, numbered from 0 to 6, but we have not used location 0. The candidates are numbered from 1 to 6 and it is natural to use array locations with the same numbers for the counts. In the first section of the program these six locations of VotesFor are initialized to zero using sequential access. Prior to doing this, these locations will contain completely unpredictable values. In the second section each number typed in from the list determines which of the six locations is to be incremented – random access. The third section finds the candidate or candidates with the highest vote count. Two loops are necessary for this, the first to find the highest total and the second to print the numbers of any candidates who have achieved this total – there may be more than one, with a tie for first place.

PROGRAM 9.8

Six candidates in an election have reference numbers 1, 2, 3, 4, 5 and 6. A list of votes takes the form of a list of such reference numbers (terminated by –1). For example:

Number typed

5	means 1 vote for candidate 5
3	means 1 vote for candidate 3
1	means 1 vote for candidate 1
3	means 1 more vote for candidate 3
⋮	
–1	means 'end of list'

The program counts the votes for each candidate and finds the winner.

```c
/* Program 9.8 : Votes */
#include <stdio.h>
void main(void)
{
  int VotesFor[7];  /*  Location 0 will not be used  */
  int candidate, MostVotesSoFar;

  /*  Set counts to 0:  */
  for (candidate = 1; candidate <= 6; candidate++)
    VotesFor[candidate] = 0;

  /*  Add up votes:  */
  scanf("%i", &candidate);
  while (candidate != -1)
  {
    VotesFor[candidate]++;
    scanf("%i", &candidate);
  }

  /*  Find winner:  */
  MostVotesSoFar = 0;
  for (candidate = 1; candidate <= 6; candidate++)
    if (VotesFor[candidate] > MostVotesSoFar)
      MostVotesSoFar = VotesFor[candidate];

  printf("\nWinner(s) is/are:");
  for (candidate = 1; candidate <= 6; candidate++)
    if (VotesFor[candidate] == MostVotesSoFar)
      printf(" %i", candidate);

  printf("\n\n");
}
```

Up until now, the subscripts of the slots of an array have corresponded naturally to integers. However, it is occasionally convenient to use values that are not integers for subscripting an array. In Program 9.9, for example, we use an array whose subscripts correspond with the 26 letters of the alphabet. The array is of size 26, and the subscripts 0 and 25 correspond to 'a' and 'z', respectively. If we know that a given character is a lower-case letter of the alphabet, we can convert it into an integer in the range 0 to 25 by 'subtracting' the character 'a'.

=========================== **PROGRAM 9.9** ===========================

This program plots a histogram showing the frequency of occurrence of each alphabetic character in a file of text. We assume that no scaling is necessary in the histogram.

```c
/* Program 9.9 : Frequency Count */

#include <stdio.h>
#include <ctype.h>

void main(void)
{
    int LetterCount[26];
    char letter, character;
    int col;
    FILE *text;

    for (letter = 0; letter <= 25; letter++)
        LetterCount[letter] = 0;

    text = fopen("TEXT.DAT","r");
    character = getc(text);

    while (!feof(text))
    {
        if ( ('a' <= character) && (character <= 'z') )
            LetterCount[character - 'a']++;
        else if ( ('A' <= character) && (character <= 'Z') )
            LetterCount[character - 'A']++;

        character = getc(text);
    }
    fclose(text);

    for (letter = 0; letter <= 25; letter++)
    {
        printf("\n");
        for (col = 0; col < LetterCount[letter]; col++)
            printf("*");
    }
    printf("\n");
}
```

Apart from this complication, the structure of the first two loops in Program 9.9 corresponds closely to the structure of the first two loops used for vote counting in Program 9.8.

Program 9.10 illustrates an alternative method of solution, using an array, for Exercise 9, Chapter 6. In this program the initialization of DaysIn is achieved by a switch statement inside a for loop. The for loop controls the sequential access and the switch statement selects the appropriate value for each location. The months are numbered 1 to 12 so it is natural to use array locations numbered 1 to 12 to

PROGRAM 9.10

This program reads two dates, each in the form day, month, and calculates the number of days from one day to the next. It is assumed that the dates are sensible and that they lie in the same year, which is not a leap year.

```c
/* Program 9.10 : Days */

#include <stdio.h>

void main(void)
{
    int month, DaysToGo, FirstDay,
        FirstMonth, SecondDay, SecondMonth;
    int DaysIn[13];

    for (month=1; month<=12; month++)
        switch (month)
        {
            case 2:             DaysIn[month] = 28; break;
            case 9: case 4:
            case 6: case 11: DaysIn[month] = 30; break;
            default:            DaysIn[month] = 31; break;
        }

    scanf("%i%i", &FirstDay, &FirstMonth);
    scanf("%i%i", &SecondDay, &SecondMonth);

    if (FirstMonth == SecondMonth)
        DaysToGo = SecondDay - FirstDay;
    else
    {
        DaysToGo = DaysIn[FirstMonth] - FirstDay; /* 1st month */
        for (month = FirstMonth+1; month < SecondMonth; month++)
            DaysToGo = DaysToGo + DaysIn[month]; /* months between */
        DaysToGo = DaysToGo + SecondDay; /* 2nd month */
    };

    printf("Days to go: %i\n", DaysToGo);
}
```

correspond to the months. Array location 0 is again not used. If the two days are not in the same month then the program calculates the number of days to go by adding three fragments to DaysToGo. For example, if the input was:

```
 5    2
20    5
```

the program would calculate the result as follows:

```
0 │    │
1 │ 31 │
2 │ 28 │⟩  DaysToGo = DaysIn[2] - FirstDay;
  │    │      (23 in this case)
3 │ 31 │⟩  for (month = FirstMonth+1; month < SecondMonth; month++)
  │    │      DaysToGo = DaysToGo + DaysIn[month];
4 │ 30 │
5 │ 31 │⟩  DaysToGo = DaysToGo + SecondDay;
  │    │      (20 in this case)
```

We could have abbreviated Program 9.10 by initializing the DaysIn array in its declaration. If we do this we must remember that the first value in our initialization list will be put in location 0 and, if location 0 is not being used, a dummy value must be provided:

```
int DaysIn[13] = {0,31,28,31,30,31,30,31,31,30,31,30,31};
```

9.6 ■ Array parameters

In this section, we describe how an array can be used as the parameter of a function. To introduce the techniques required, consider the following simple problem.

Freda and Joe have each taken six examination papers. Write a program that will read the six marks obtained by Freda followed by the six marks obtained by Joe. The program should calculate the total marks obtained by each candidate and should then print the six individual paper marks and the total mark for each candidate. The marks for the candidate with the higher total mark should be printed first. An outline structure for this program is as follows:

```
void main(void)
{ int FredasMarks[6], JoesMarks[6];
  int FredasTotal, JoesTotal;

  Read Freda's marks and add them up;
  Read Joe's marks and add them up;
```

```
if (FredasTotal > JoesTotal)
{ printf("Freda: "); writeout(FredasMarks, FredasTotal);
  printf("Joe:  "); writeout(JoesMarks,  JoesTotal); }
else
{ printf("Joe:  "); writeout(JoesMarks,  JoesTotal);
  printf("Freda: "); writeout(FredasMarks, FredasTotal); }
}
```

The process of reading and adding Freda's marks will be very similar to the process of reading and adding Joe's marks. The only difference will be that the marks for the two candidates will be stored in two different arrays and the totals in two different variables. We therefore define a C function to read and add a candidate's marks. The function will need to be given two parameters, an array for storing the marks and a variable in which to accumulate the total.

For example, the function call:

```
ReadAndAdd(FredasMarks, &FredasTotal);
```

will read six numbers into the array `FredasMarks` and add these numbers together, putting the total in `FredasTotal`. This function will be defined in terms of two parameters – an array of six locations and an integer variable. When we wish to call a function with an array as a parameter, we simply give the name of the array in the function call – `FredasMarks` in this case. The function definition needs to be as follows:

```
void ReadAndAdd(int MarkFor[], int *total)
{ int NextPaper;
  *total = 0;
  for (NextPaper = 0; NextPaper <= 5; NextPaper++)
  {
    scanf("%i", &(MarkFor[NextPaper]) );
    *total += MarkFor[NextPaper];
  }
}
```

We indicate that a dummy parameter is an array by including the square brackets after its name. When the function is passed the name of an actual array as above, it is always given the address of that array as mentioned in Section 9.3. The contents of that array are then available to be used or altered by the function. You must not use the addressing operator `&` when supplying an actual array parameter, whether or not it will be altered by the function.

The complete program is presented as Program 9.11.

================ **PROGRAM 9.11** ================

```c
/* Program 9.11 : Exam */

#include <stdio.h>

void ReadAndAdd(int MarkFor[], int *total);
void writeout(int MarkFor[], int total);

void main(void)
{ int FredasMarks[6], JoesMarks[6];
  int FredasTotal, JoesTotal;

  ReadAndAdd(FredasMarks, &FredasTotal);
  ReadAndAdd(JoesMarks,  &JoesTotal );
  if (FredasTotal > JoesTotal)
  {
    printf("Freda: "); writeout(FredasMarks, FredasTotal);
    printf("Joe:  "); writeout(JoesMarks,  JoesTotal);
  }
  else
  {
    printf("Joe:  "); writeout(JoesMarks,  JoesTotal);
    printf("Freda: "); writeout(FredasMarks, FredasTotal);
  }
}

void ReadAndAdd(int MarkFor[], int *total)
{ int NextPaper;
  *total = 0;
  for (NextPaper = 0; NextPaper <= 5; NextPaper++)
  {
    scanf("%i", &(MarkFor[NextPaper]) );
    *total += MarkFor[NextPaper];
  }
}

void writeout(int MarkFor[], int total)
{
  int NextPaper;
  for (NextPaper = 0; NextPaper <= 5; NextPaper++)
    printf("%3i", MarkFor[NextPaper]);
  printf("   total %i\n", total);
}
```

9.7 ■ Two-dimensional arrays

Many techniques in science, engineering and commerce deal with data that is organized in two dimensions. Digitized pictures from many sources are enhanced and manipulated by computer. The pictures are represented inside the computer as a two-dimensional table of numbers. Each number corresponds to the brightness or colour of a picture element or point. A picture is converted into a table of numbers by a special input device and, after it is processed, it is converted back into a picture by a special output device. It is much easier and more natural for a programmer to think in terms of a two-dimensional set of picture elements – the picture retaining its two-dimensional form when referred to in the program – than it would be if the picture elements were strung out row-wise or column-wise into a one-dimensional array or list.

Consider another example – an 8×10 table of numbers (8 rows, 10 columns), where each number represents the population of the corresponding zone of an 8×10 square mile map. We can retain the two-dimensional nature of the data by storing it in a two-dimensional array PopMap. First of all, let us see how we declare such an array.

```
int PopMap[8][10];
```

This declaration has set up a two-dimensional structure of integer variables into which we can place the data. It is usual to picture a two-dimensional array as a collection of variables, all of the same type, organized into rows and columns, as shown in Figure 9.1, where the first subscript determines a row and the second subscript determines a column. For example, PopMap[2][6] refers to the location in the third row and the seventh column of the array. Thus, the declared array corresponds in size and shape to the table of data that we are considering.

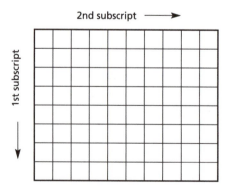

Figure 9.1 A two-dimensional array organized into rows and columns.

To do something systematically with all of the locations of a two-dimensional array, we need to use a nested `for` loop. For example, if we wish to deal with the array a row at a time we need the outline structure:

```
for (row = 0; row <= 7; row++)
      Deal with row;
```

and dealing with a row involves a further loop:

```
for (column = 0; column <= 9; column++)
      Deal with the location PopMap[row][column];
```

Program 9.12 illustrates this.

━━━━━━━━━━━━━━━━━━━━━ **PROGRAM 9.12** ━━━━━━━━━━━━━━━━━━━━━

This program reads the population table described above, stores it in a suitable array, calculates the total population and prints a copy of the population table.

```
/* Program 9.12 : Population */
#include <stdio.h>
void main(void)
{
   int PopMap[8][10];
   int row, column, total;
   FILE *populate;
   populate = fopen("POPULATE.DAT", "r");
   for (row = 0; row <= 7; row++)
   for (column = 0; column <= 9; column++)
      fscanf(populate, "%i", &(PopMap[row][column]) );
   fclose(populate);
   total = 0;
   for (row = 0; row <= 7; row++)
      for (column = 0; column <= 9; column++)
         total += PopMap[row][column];
   printf("Total population is %i.\n", total);
   printf("Populations of individual zones are:\n");
   for (row = 0; row <= 7; row++)
   {
      printf("\n");
      for (column = 0; column <= 9; column++)
         printf("%4i", PopMap[row][column]);
   }
   printf("\n");
}
```

The first nested `for` loop causes the data to be read into the two-dimensional array `PopMap`, the second accesses the array, performing the required calculation, and the third causes the contents of the array to be printed. In the file containing the input for Program 9.12, the 10 numbers in the first row of the table appear first and these are read into row 0 of the array. The next 10 numbers in the file are read into row 1 of the array, and so on. Incidentally, the processes of reading the data and accumulating the total could have been carried out simultaneously, the first two nested loops being merged into a single nested loop:

```
total = 0;
for (row = 0; row <= 7; row++)
    for (column = 0; column <= 9; column++)
    {
        scanf("%i", &(PopMap[row][column]) );
        total += PopMap[row][column];
    }
```

In Program 9.13, the user specifies a sub-region of the map in which the total population is required. The complete map is read before this sub-region can be conveniently accessed.

═══════════ **PROGRAM 9.13** ═══════════

This program reads data from a file, as in Program 9.12. In addition it reads, from the keyboard, four numbers defining a sub-region on the map over which the population is to be added. For example, input of 2 6 3 5 specifies the region lying between rows 2 and 6 and between columns 3 and 5 (rows and columns are again numbered from 0), as shown in Figure 9.2.

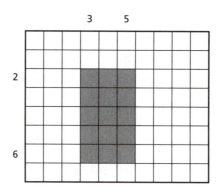

Figure 9.2 Defining a sub-region of a map.

```
/* Program 9.13 : PopMap 2 */

#include <stdio.h>

void main(void)
{
    int PopMap[8][10];
    int row, col, rowA, colA, rowB, colB, SubTotal;
    FILE *PopFile;
    PopFile = fopen("POPULATE.DAT", "r");

    for (row = 0; row <= 7; row++)
        for (col = 0; col <= 9; col++)
            fscanf(PopFile,"%i", &(PopMap[row][col]) );

    fclose(PopFile);

    SubTotal = 0;
    scanf("%i%i%i%i", &rowA, &rowB, &colA, & colB);

    for (row = rowA; row <= rowB; row++)
        for (col = colA; col <= colB; col++)
            SubTotal += PopMap[row][col];

    printf("Population of sub-zone is %i.\n", SubTotal);

}
```

Program 9.14 illustrates random access to a two-dimensional array. Information about a two-dimensional lecture timetable is built up gradually from information about the individual lectures, which is supplied in an unpredictable order.

In the specification of Program 9.14, the days are numbered from 1 to 5 and the periods are numbered from 1 to 6. It is natural to reflect this in our data structure and to ignore row 0 and column 0 of the timetable array.

PROGRAM 9.14

A student's week is divided up into five days, each of six periods numbered 1–6. Student must attend 20 lectures during each week. The program reads a list of the student's lecture times and places. Each lecture time is represented by two integers giving the day (1–5) and the period (1–6), and these two integers are followed by the number of the room (a positive integer) in which the lecture takes place.

The program prints a timetable for the student in the form:

```
             Period
       1   2   3   4   5   6
      -----------------------
Mon   3   1   2   9
Tue   6   6   5   7   6
Wed       2   1
Thu   5   2   5           8   7
Fri   3   2   1   3
```

where the entry for each period represents the room number in which the lecture is held. We assume that the input data is such that there are no timetable clashes.

```c
/* Program 9.14 : Times */

#include <stdio.h>

void main(void)
{
   int day, period, room, lecture;
   int place[6][7];

   /* Use zeros to mark all periods as free */
   for (day = 1; day <= 5; day++)
      for (period = 1; period <= 6; period++)
         place[day][period] = 0;

   /* Now fill in appropriate periods with room number */

   for (lecture = 1; lecture <= 20; lecture++)
   {
      scanf("%i%i%i", &day, &period, &room);
      place[day][period] = room;
   }

   /* Now print the timetable */

   printf("             Period\n\n");
   printf("        1 2 3 4 5 6\n");
   printf("       ----------------\n");

   for (day = 1; day <= 5; day++)
   {
      switch(day)
      {
         case 1: printf("Mon"); break;
         case 2: printf("Tue"); break;
         case 3: printf("Wed"); break;
         case 4: printf("Thu"); break;
         case 5: printf("Fri"); break;
```

```
          }
          for (period = 1; period <= 6; period++)
          {
              if (place[day][period] == 0) printf("   ");
              else printf("%3i", place[day][period]);
          }
          printf("\n");
      }
  }
```

SUMMARY OF CHAPTER 9

Key points

- Arrays allow us to use a single name for a collection of variables. We refer to the individual variables with a numeric subscript.
- Before an array has been initialized, do not make any assumptions about the contents of its elements.
- A `for` loop allows us to access all of an array's elements in sequence.
- Sometimes it is more natural to ignore slot zero of an array.
- A nested `for` loop allows us to access all of a two-dimensional array's elements.
- The addressing operator is not used when passing an array to a function as a reference parameter.

Common problems	
Problem	**Symptom**
Array subscripts that go out of range.	Program will attempt to access or store data elsewhere in the computer memory, corrupting other variables or even system software.
Forgetting that the last slot in an array has a subscript that is one less than the array size.	This usually results in using a subscript that is out of range – see above.
Reading or copying strings into arrays that are not big enough.	As above.

Problem *(continued)*	Symptom *(continued)*
Using %s to read a string that contains spaces.	Only part of the string will be read.
Using gets to read a string that finishes before the end of the line of data.	Too many characters will be read into the string, and all subsequent data will be out of step.
Confusion between rows and columns in a two-dimensional array.	Program will access the wrong slot or the wrong data.

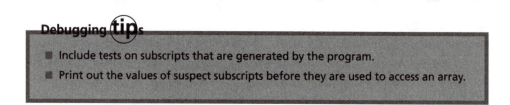

Debugging **tips**

- Include tests on subscripts that are generated by the program.
- Print out the values of suspect subscripts before they are used to access an array.

EXERCISES FOR CHAPTER 9

(1) Write a program similar to Program 9.2 but which reads a price list for 100 items from a file. The program is then to read a list of quantities required by a customer; for example:

```
12    means 12 of item  0
5     means  5 of item  1
10    means 10 of item  2
0     means  0 of item  3
 :
 :
27    means 27 of item 99
```

The program should calculate the total cost of the customer's order.

(2) As Exercise 1, but this time the customer's order is specified as a list of pairs, where each pair contains an item number followed by the quantity required. The list can be terminated by a pair of negative numbers. The item numbers appear in any order. The program should check that each item number input does in fact exist.

(3) Write a program that reads a piece of text terminated by a '*' and finds the most frequently occurring letter in the text.

(4) Write a program that will read an integer n followed by an *n*-letter word and that will determine whether or not the word is a palindrome. (A palindrome is a word that reads the same forwards and backwards, for example 'rotor'.)

(5) Write a program that accepts input from a file of thirty daily temperature readings in the range –20 to 40. The program is to draw a graph of the following form:

```
1                    +    *
2                    +  *
3                  *+
4              *    +
5                  *+
6                +    *
7                +      *
    etc.
```

where the distance of a '*' from the left represents a temperature reading and the position of the '+'s represents the average reading over the whole period.

(6) Each day in a college's weekly timetable is divided into seven periods. The timetable for a course consists of a list of five periods during which the course is given, where a period is represented by two numbers, the first giving the day of the week (1 = Monday, 2 = Tuesday, etc.) and the second giving the number of the period on that day. Write a program that accepts as input the timetables for the six courses a student wishes to attend. The program should report whether there are any timetable clashes and, if so, when.

(7) The measurement of various parts of a fingerprint results in a sequence of ten floating point values. Two such sets of measurements can be compared by counting the number of corresponding pairs of values that differ by less than 5% of the larger value. Two fingerprints are classified as similar if this comparison results in a count of seven or more. Write a program that reads a set of measurements for one fingerprint found on the scene of a crime and then compares that fingerprint with the fingerprints of known criminals, whose measurements are to be read as further input. For comparing two sets of fingerprint measurements, your program should use a 'logical' (int) function that can be used as follows:

```
if (similar(FoundPrint, KnownPrint)) ...
```

(8) A particular photomicrograph contains a single simple convex shape, such as a circle, represented as a dark area on a light background. Such images are commonly represented in computers as two-dimensional arrays, where each element has the value 1 or 0. A dark area on a light background becomes a group of 1s surrounded by 0s.

Write a program that will accept such an array as input. The program should display the shape of the dark region by printing the points on the boundary as 1s and the background and interior points as spaces. Test your program on a 10 × 10 array.

➡ **Hint:** Scan the image row-wise or column-wise. For a given 1, if any of the surrounding points are 0s, then that 1 represents a boundary point.

(9) The output from a black-and-white television camera is a sequence of pictures, and each picture can be digitized as an array of 400×600 integers, each integer indicating the brightness of one point on the picture.

Write a program that reads digitized pictures taken alternately from two cameras. The first camera is directed at a brightly lit object moving against a very dark background. A point on the background appears in a picture as a brightness value less than 5. The output from the program is to be a sequence of digitized pictures from the second camera with the brightly lit object from the first camera superimposed.

It might be convenient to test your program on smaller pictures, of size 4×6, say.

(10) Write a program that will play a game of noughts and crosses against someone at the keyboard. The person at the keyboard can specify a move by typing the number of the square in which he or she wants to play. A simple version of the program could make its move by playing in the first empty square it finds. The program should terminate and print an appropriate message as soon as one of the players wins.

CHAPTER 10

Collections of values: Structures

Until now, we have used a variable to contain a single value, or, in the case of an array, a collection of values (all of the same type) indexed by number. In this chapter, we introduce a new way of grouping values together using something called a **structure** (not to be confused with control structures).

We use a structure when we want to group a number of components together in one entity. A structure differs from an array in two major ways: firstly, its components are named rather than numbered; secondly, the components within a structure need not all be of the same type.

We shall refer to the components which make up a structure as its **members**, but it is worth noting that this terminology is quite specific to the C programming language. What C calls 'a structure and its members', another programming language might refer to as 'a record and its fields'. 'Record' and 'field' would certainly be preferred in a general discussion of database systems.

10.1 ■ Simple structures

As a first example of structures, suppose we wished to manage a database of books in a bookshop. For the moment, we shall record for each book its year of publication and retail price. This would require a structure **type declaration** as follows:

```
typedef struct {
    int year;
    float price;
} books;
```

It is important to note that this does not declare a variable called books, nor for that matter does it declare variables named year and price. The statement specifies a new data type called books, which can subsequently be used to declare variables in just the same way as int, float and char. Using this defined type, we can declare:

```
books zen, poker;
```

This creates two separate structure variables called zen and poker, which can be visualized as:

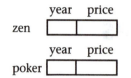

Each variable has an internal structure which reflects the definition of the type books – each variable contains space for two values, an int called year and a float called price.

How can we access the internal slots or members of one of these structures if they are both contained in a variable with just one name? To do this, we use the dot notation. For example, we can put values into the above structures with the following assignment statements:

```
zen.year = 1974;
zen.price = 4.99;

poker.year = 1957;
poker.price = 5.95;
```

Obeying these statements produces the situation:

```
        year    price
zen    | 1974 |  4.99 |

        year    price
poker  | 1957 |  5.95 |
```

The values inserted into these variables can then be used in the same way as the values stored in any other variables. For example, the statement:

```
printf("The book on Zen was published in %i and costs %.2f",
                                    zen.year, zen.price);
```

will produce the output:

```
The book on Zen was published in 1974 and costs 4.99
```

Why do we group values together in this way? The first reason is a practical one. If we had avoided the use of structures altogether in the above example, we would have had to use something like:

```
int ZenYear, PokerYear;
float ZenPrice, PokerPrice;

ZenYear = 1974;
ZenPrice = 4.99;

PokerYear = 1957;
PokerPrice = 5.95;
```

Although at first glance this might appear simpler, it is important to note that it contains twice as many variable declarations as the structure version. If the structure for representing a book was more realistic, with other components such as book title, author name, quantity in stock, and so on, we would still need only two variable declarations for two books. Many more would be required if structures were not used.

A second reason, which might seem rather philosophical but which has practical implications, is as follows: sometimes we want to refer to and manipulate the whole without worrying about its constituent parts. For instance, in moving your car from A to B, you would not consider doing so component by component. You would move an entity called 'car', which happens to be made up of elements such as 'engine', 'wheels', and so on. Grouping things together in this way is sometimes known as **encapsulation**.

In our first example, we stored two values for each book variable. Of course, a structure is not limited to contain just two members – if, for example, we also wish to record the number of pages for each book, the following definition of books is perfectly acceptable:

```
typedef struct {
    int year;
    float price;
    int pages;
} books;
```

which might be used in the body of our program as follows:

```
books zen, poker;

zen.year = 1974
zen.price = 4.99;
zen.pages = 400;

poker.year = 1957
poker.price = 5.95;
poker.pages = 160;
```

Pictorially we have:

	year	price	pages
zen	1974	4.99	400

	year	price	pages
poker	1957	5.95	160

Here, we have not declared any new variables, but the new member pages is available in both existing variables – meaning that six values are stored in total (three for each book). Without the use of structures, we would have had to declare a new variable for each book (just two variables in this case, but ten variables if we were dealing with ten books, and so on).

Although in these introductory examples, we have used just `float` and `int` members within a structure, the members can be of any type – integer, floating point, character; a member can even be an array or another (previously defined) structure. In this way, large and complex data structures can be built up from the basic types provided.

In Program 10.1, we have extended our simple definition of the `books` type to contain a member called `title`, which is in fact an array of characters, or string as introduced in Chapter 9, Section 9.3. Note the use of the `strcpy` function to copy a constant string into a character array. Each string has room for up to 50 characters plus the end of string marker.

PROGRAM 10.1

This program creates and assigns structure variables for two books and displays information about the books on the screen.

```c
/* Program 10.1 : Introducing structs */
#include <stdio.h>
#include <string.h>

typedef struct {
  char title[51];
  int year;
  float price;
} books;

void main (void) {

  books zen, poker;

  strcpy(zen.title,"Zen and the Art of Motorcycle Maintenance");
  zen.year = 1974;
  zen.price = 4.99;

  strcpy(poker.title,"The Education of a Poker Player");
  poker.year = 1957;
  poker.price = 5.95;

  printf("%s was published in %i and costs %.2f\n",
                      zen.title, zen.year, zen.price);
  printf("%s was published in %i and costs %.2f\n",
                      poker.title, poker.year, poker.price);

}
```

10.2 ■ Tables: Arrays of structures

It is uncommon to find a single structured variable floating around on its own – typically we group a set of data items into a structure when we have a large number of similar structures to deal with. A collection of many items, each of which can be broken down in the same way, is best treated as an array of structures. Recall how the declaration for a single integer variable can be made into an array declaration by appending a number in square brackets to the declaration.

```
int myarray[5];
```

Similarly, we can declare an array of structures. For example, using the type definition of books from Program 10.1, we might have:

```
books book[5];
```

This declares an array of five entities, each of which has the type books. Such an array of structures is often called a **table**. We can visualize this array as:

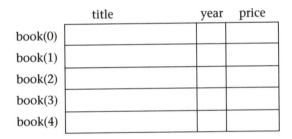

	title	year	price
book(0)			
book(1)			
book(2)			
book(3)			
book(4)			

The individual members of the structures in the array might be accessed by statements such as:

```
strcpy(book[2].title,"Simple Pascal");
book[2].year = 1981;
book[2].price = 14.99;
printf("Year of publication of book 2 is %i\n",book[2].year);
```

As you see, the use of a singular noun 'book' for the name of the array reads better when it is used in this type of context.

A typical scenario in which we use a table will involve reading data into the table from a file, performing some operations on the table and then possibly writing a revised version of the table to a new file.

Program 10.2 illustrates the simple use of a table of structures.

══════════════ **PROGRAM 10.2** ══════════════

This program reads a simple table of book data from a text file and then prints
the list on screen, with an asterisk preceding the titles of the books that have the
most recent year of publication.

```c
/* Program 10.2 : Latest books */

#include <stdio.h>

typedef struct {
  char title [51];
  int year;
  float price;
} books;

FILE *BookFile;
books book[21];
int LastBook;

void LoadBookFile (void);

void main (void)
{
  int index, LatestYear;

  LoadBookFile();
  LatestYear = book[1].year;
  for (index = 2; index <= LastBook; index++)
    if (book[index].year > LatestYear)
      LatestYear = book[index].year;

  for (index = 1; index <= LastBook; index++)
  {
    if (book[index].year == LatestYear)
      printf ("*");
    else
      printf (" ");

    printf ("%3i. ", index);

    printf ("%s %4i %7.2f\n", book[index].title,
      book[index].year, book[index].price );
  }

}

void LoadBookFile (void)
{
  char NextChar;
  int NextFree, i, year;
  float price;
```

```
BookFile = fopen("BOOKS.DAT", "r");
NextFree = 1;
NextChar = getc(BookFile);

while (!feof(BookFile) && NextFree <= 20)
{
    book[NextFree].title[0] = NextChar;
    for (i = 1; i <= 49; i++)
      book[NextFree].title [i] = fgetc(BookFile);
    book[NextFree].title [50] = '\0';
    fscanf ( BookFile, "%i %f", &year, &price);
    book[NextFree].year = year;
    book[NextFree].price = price;
    NextFree++;
    do {
      NextChar = getc(BookFile);
    } while ( NextChar != '\n' && !feof(BookFile) );
    NextChar = getc(BookFile);
}
LastBook = NextFree - 1;
fclose(BookFile);
}
```

The program initializes the array from a text file, which might look like this:

Zen and the Art of Motorcycle Maintenance	1974	4.99
The Education of a Poker Player	1957	5.95
The Physics of Vibrations and Waves	1961	9.99
Chambers 20th Century Thesaurus	1983	21.99
The Ginger Man	1956	3.95
Reflections on the Revolution in France	1790	157.00
Pascal for Science and Engineering	1983	19.99
The 35mm Photographer's Handbook	1979	15.95

If the file contains more than 20 entries, only the first 20 will be used, and titles of books are assumed to be exactly 50 characters long in the file.

The loop that reads the structures from the text file into the array detects the end of the file by reading one character from the start of the next line of data prior to each cycle of the loop. The end of the file can then be detected easily, when it occurs, by feof.

The string representing a book title is read character by character into the title member of the structure and the end of string marker '\0' is explicitly placed at the end of the string array. This is necessary in order that printf and %s can later recognize the end of the stored string.

10.3 ■ Structures compared with other variable types

Just as one integer can be given the value of another:

```
int a, b;
    .
    .
    .
a = b;
```

the contents of one structured variable can be copied into another. When such an assignment takes place, every member in the structured variable on the left-hand side is set to the value from the corresponding member of the variable on the right-hand side.

================ PROGRAM 10.3 ================

This program swaps the information in the two structure variables MyPair and YourPair.

```
/* Program 10.3 : Swap Shoes */

typedef struct {
   char sex;
   int size;
} shoes;

void main (void)
{
   shoes MyPair, YourPair, temp;

   MyPair.sex = 'M';
   MyPair.size = 11;

   YourPair.sex = 'F';
   YourPair.size = 8;

   printf("My shoes are: %c %i.\n", MyPair.sex, MyPair.size);
   printf("Your shoes are: %c %i.\n", YourPair.sex, YourPair.size);

   temp = YourPair;
   YourPair = MyPair;
   MyPair = temp;

   printf("Now my shoes are: %c %i.\n", MyPair.sex, MyPair.size);
   printf("Now your shoes are: %c %i.\n", YourPair.sex, YourPair.size);

}
```

So in Program 10.3, the line:

```
temp = YourPair;
```

is a concise and useful way of saying:

```
temp.sex = YourPair.sex;
temp.size = YourPair.size;
```

Assignment between two structs is allowed only if they are of exactly the same type. The following is not acceptable:

```
typedef struct { int year; float price; } books;
typedef struct { char sex; int size; } shoes;

    .
    .
    .

books FairyTale;
shoes slippers;

    .
    .
    .

FairyTale = slippers;
```

Less obviously, the following is also *not* acceptable:

```
typedef struct { int year; float price; } booksA;
typedef struct { int year; float price; } booksB;

    .
    .
    .

booksA FairyTale;
booksB fable;

    .
    .
    .

FairyTale = fable;
```

As far as the computer is concerned, booksA and booksB are two different types.

In the last example, structured variables behaved in much the same way as simple variables such as integers. This might lead us to expect that comparison of structure variables is also acceptable – recall that with two integers we can write:

```
if (integer1 == integer2) ...
```

to test for equality. With structures this is not the case, even when the variables are of exactly the same struct type. For example, the following would cause a compiler error:

```
    .
    .
    .

books a, b;
    .
    .
    .

if (a == b) printf("same book");
```

For structures we must define our own notion of what constitutes equality; per-haps we wish to test whether every member of a structure is identical to the corresponding member in another structure, or perhaps we wish to test for equal-ity in just one member, as follows:

```
if (zen.year == poker.year))
   printf("These were published in the same year\n");
```

10.4 ■ Structures as parameters

Something else we can do with a simple variable is pass it as a parameter to a func-tion. In the same way, it is possible to pass a complete structure variable to a function. In Program 10.4, the structured variable zen is passed to a function which simply displays its price – the contents of the price member in the structure. Note that in the function declaration, the parameter is declared as being of type books – our user-defined type.

PROGRAM 10.4

This example prints the price of a book by passing a structure to a function.

```
/* Program 10.4 : Passing a struct to a function */

#include <stdio.h>

typedef struct {
   int pages;
   float price;
} books;

void ShowPrice ( books SomeBook );

void main (void)
{
   books zen;
   zen.pages = 400;
   zen.price = 4.99;
   printf("Zen costs ");
   ShowPrice(zen);
}

void ShowPrice ( books SomeBook )
{
   printf("%.2f\n", SomeBook.price);
}
```

It is also perfectly acceptable to *return* a structure from a function. We must simply declare the function as being of the appropriate type. Given the structure type declaration:

```
typedef struct { int day; int month; int year; } dates;
```

the following function takes a parameter representing one date and returns a structure that represents the date of the next day. (We have avoided the complication of leap years and assume that February always has 28 days.)

```
dates NextDay (dates GivenDate)
{ dates NewDate;
   int DaysIn[13] = {0,31,28,31,30,31,30,31,31,30,31,30,31};

   NewDate.day = GivenDate.day + 1;

   if (NewDate.day > DaysIn[GivenDate.month])
   {
      NewDate.day = 1;
      NewDate.month = GivenDate.month + 1;
   }
   else NewDate.month = GivenDate.month;

   if (NewDate.month > 12)
   {
      NewDate.month = 1;
      NewDate.year = GivenDate.year + 1;
   }
   else NewDate.year = GivenDate.year;

   return NewDate;
}
```

This could be called with, for example:

```
dates today, tomorrow;

printf("Give today's date:");
scanf("%i%i%i", &today.day, &today.month, &today.year);

tomorrow = NextDay(today);
```

Suppose now that in Program 10.4 we wish to write a function which, instead of displaying the price of a book, increases that value by 10%. We might try to write the function as follows:

```
void RaisePrice ( books SomeBook )
{
   SomeBook.price = 1.1 * SomeBook.price;
}
```

However, when we make a call to this function such as

```
RaisePrice (zen);
```

within the body of main, the variable zen is unchanged by the call. Only the local copy of the parameter inside the function body is affected.

One way to achieve our desired result might be to write a function which, as well as accepting a parameter of type books, returns a value of type books with the appropriate member increased. Then, in main, we can write

```
zen = RaisePrice (zen);
```

to update the variable zen.

Alternatively, we could write a void function whose parameter is a reference parameter, as introduced in Chapter 7, Section 7.3. This is demonstrated in Program 10.5. The use of parentheses round the references to the structure parameter (*SomeBook) is essential because of the relative precedences of the * and dot operators.

PROGRAM 10.5

This program raises the price of a book twice, and tells us the new price.

```
/* Program 10.5 : Price raise */

#include <stdio.h>

typedef struct {
    int pages;
    float price;
} books;

void RaisePrice ( books *SomeBook );

void main (void) {
    books zen;
    zen.pages = 400;
    zen.price = 4.99;
    printf ("Zen costs: %.2f\n", zen.price);
    RaisePrice(&zen);
    RaisePrice(&zen);
    printf ("Zen now costs: %.2f\n", zen.price);
}

void RaisePrice ( books *SomeBook )
{
    (*SomeBook).price = 1.1 * (*SomeBook).price;
}
```

10.4 ■ Searching in tables

A commonly used operation in a table is the search for a particular item of data.

In Program 10.6, we use our table of book structures to demonstrate a simple search. In computing, a 'search' is just what one would expect – we are going to look through a series of items (in this case, elements in an array) until we find one which satisfies certain criteria. Here we are searching through a simple bookshop database for any book satisfying some condition. In this case, the search conditions are very simple – in realistic examples, they could be much more elaborate.

═══════ **PROGRAM 10.6** ═══════

This program reads a table of books from a file and then repeatedly presents a simple menu of options to the user. From the menu, the user can search for books published in a given year, search for books cheaper than a given price, or indicate that no further searches are required.

```c
/* Program 10.6 : Book search */

#include <stdio.h>

#define TRUE 1
#define FALSE 0

typedef struct {
   char title [51];
   int year;
   float price;
} books;

FILE *BookFile;
books book[21];
int LastBook;

void LoadBookFile (void);
void LoadNextBook (books *onebook);
void DisplayMenu (void);
void SearchByYear (void);
void SearchByPrice (void);
void DisplayOneBook (books b);

void main (void)
{
   int command;
   LoadBookFile();
   do {
      DisplayMenu();
      scanf ("%i", &command);
      if (command == 1) SearchByYear();
      if (command == 2) SearchByPrice();
   } while (command != 3);
}
```

```
void LoadBookFile (void)
{
  int NextFree;
  books BookBuffer;
  BookFile = fopen("BOOKS.DAT", "r");
  NextFree = 1;
  LoadNextBook (&BookBuffer);
  while (!feof(BookFile) && NextFree <= 20)
  {
    book[NextFree] = BookBuffer;
    NextFree++;
    LoadNextBook (&BookBuffer);
  }
  LastBook = NextFree - 1;
  fclose(BookFile);
}

void LoadNextBook (books *onebook)
{
  int i, ch;
  int year;
  float price;

  for (i = 0; i <= 49; i++)
    (*onebook).title [i] = getc(BookFile);
  (*onebook).title [50] = '\0';

  fscanf (BookFile, "%i %f", &year, &price);

  (*onebook).year = year;
  (*onebook).price = price;

  do {
    ch = getc(BookFile);
  } while ( ch != '\n' && !feof(BookFile) );
}

void DisplayMenu (void)
{
  printf ("\n");
  printf ("1: Search by year\n");
  printf ("2: Search by price\n");
  printf ("3: Quit\n");
  printf ("Enter selection: ");
}
```

```
void SearchByYear (void)
{
   int SearchYear, SearchIndex, NoBooks;
   printf ("Year of publication: "); scanf ("%i", &SearchYear);
   NoBooks = TRUE;

   for (SearchIndex = 1; SearchIndex <= LastBook; SearchIndex++)
   {
      if (book[SearchIndex].year == SearchYear)
      {
         DisplayOneBook (book[SearchIndex]);
         NoBooks = FALSE;
      }
   }

   if (NoBooks)
      printf ("There are no books published that year.\n");
}

void SearchByPrice (void)
{
   int SearchIndex, NoBooks;
   float UpperLimit;

   printf ("Upper limit for price: "); scanf ("%f", &UpperLimit);
   NoBooks = TRUE;

   for (SearchIndex = 1; SearchIndex <= LastBook; SearchIndex++)
   {
      if (book[SearchIndex].price <= UpperLimit)
      {
         DisplayOneBook (book[SearchIndex]);
         NoBooks = FALSE;
      }
   }

   if (NoBooks)
      printf ("There are no books in your price range.\n");
}

void DisplayOneBook (books b)
{
   printf ("%s %4i %3.2f\n", b.title, b.year, b.price );
}
```

The searches are very simple, and each consists of just an `if` statement within a `for` loop. Searching is a much-required operation in databases, and when speed of search in large databases is critical, clever algorithms can be used in place of the 'brute force' searches shown here.

10.5 ■ Sorting tables

Another commonly required technique when working with a database is the 'sort'. Before going into details, what do we mean by a 'sort'? Typically, we have a set of data (in this case, an array of structures again), in which one member of each item in the array (the same member for each item) can be considered a 'key'. We want to re-order the array so that its elements are arranged with the first element having the smallest of all the keys, the second element having the second-smallest key and so on, with the last element having the largest key.

There are many algorithms for sorting data. Some are specific to certain types of data or are optimized for data that is known to be 'nearly in order' or 'very disordered'. A general sorting algorithm is described here. It has the advantages of elegance and conciseness, but in a real-world situation, another algorithm might be more appropriate. For the sake of discussion, suppose we intend to sort an array containing ten book structures so that their year values are in ascending order. We shall assume that elements are numbered from 1 to 10 and we are not going to use element zero.

Sorting an array of ten entries can be achieved by first finding the entry with the largest key and placing it in position ten in the array, then finding the entry with the second-largest key (placing it in position nine), then the entry with the third largest key, and so on until all entries in the array are in the correct order.

The important thing to recognize here is that once the largest element is in its correct position (position ten), we can ignore it, and concentrate on the new problem of finding the largest of the remaining nine entries. The same is then true of the ninth element in the array – we can forget about it and move down to look at just the first eight entries. Repositioning and subsequently ignoring the element with the largest remaining key at each stage will eventually lead us to the point where all entries have been sorted.

This immediately suggests a loop structure along the lines of:

```
for (NumberToSort = 10; NumberToSort >= 2; NumberToSort -- )
{
    Look at the entries from 1 to NumberToSort and
        place the entry with the largest key in position NumberToSort
}
```

Now we need to tackle the repeated subproblem of 'Look at the entries from 1 to NumberToSort and place the entry with the largest key in position NumberToSort'.

For the sake of the example, suppose we have already found the entries with the largest and second-largest keys and they have been placed in positions ten and nine, respectively. So now NumberToSort takes the value 8, and we must somehow ensure that from the first eight entries in the array we find the one with the largest key and get it into position eight.

The obvious way to achieve this is to cycle through all eight entries, keeping a note of 'largest key so far' and 'the position in the array of the entry with that largest key'. We did something similar to this in Program 10.2. Once all the entries have been examined, we can simply get the entry with the largest key and swap it with entry 8.

This looks like this:

```
LargestKey = book[1].year;
LargestKeyWasAt = 1;
for (index = 2; index <=8; index++)
{
   if (book[index].year > LargestKey)
     {
       LargestKey = book[index].year ;
       LargestKeyWasAt = index;
     }
}
```

Swap entry 8 *with entry* LargestKeyWasAt;

All that remains is to incorporate this into the outer loop described earlier (8 gets replaced with NumberToSort) and to implement the details of how to swap a pair of entries.

═══ **PROGRAM 10.7** ═══

This program reads a database of books from a file into an array, which is then sorted by year.

```
/* Program 10.7 : Sort */

#include <stdio.h>

typedef struct {
   char title [51];
   int year;
   float price;
} books;

FILE *BookFile;
books book[21];
int LastBook;
```

```c
void LoadBookFile    (void);
void LoadNextBook (books *onebook);
void DisplayAllBooks (void);
void DisplayOneBook   (books b);
void SwapBooks (int FirstIndex, int SecondIndex);
void main(void)
{
  int NumberToSort, LargestKey, LargestKeyWasAt, index;

  LoadBookFile();
  printf("\nBefore sort:\n");
  DisplayAllBooks();

  for (NumberToSort = LastBook; NumberToSort >= 2; NumberToSort--)
  {
    LargestKey = book[1].year;
    LargestKeyWasAt = 1;
    for (index = 2; index <= NumberToSort; index++)
    {
      if (book[index].year > LargestKey)
      {
        LargestKey = book[index].year;
        LargestKeyWasAt = index;
      }
    }
    if (LargestKeyWasAt != NumberToSort)
      SwapBooks (LargestKeyWasAt, NumberToSort);
  }
  printf("\nAfter sort:\n");
  DisplayAllBooks();
}

void LoadBookFile (void)
{
  int NextFree;
  books BookBuffer;
  BookFile = fopen("BOOKS.DAT", "r");
  NextFree = 1;
  LoadNextBook (&BookBuffer);
  while (!feof(BookFile) && NextFree <= 20)
  {
    book[NextFree] = BookBuffer;
    NextFree++;
    LoadNextBook (&BookBuffer);
  }
  LastBook = NextFree - 1;
  fclose(BookFile);
}
```

```
void LoadNextBook (books *onebook)
{
   int i, ch;
   int year;
   float price;

   for (i = 0; i <= 49; i++)
      (*onebook).title [i] = getc(BookFile);
   (*onebook).title [50] = '\0';

   fscanf (BookFile, "%i %f", &year, &price);

   (*onebook).year = year;
   (*onebook).price = price;

   do {
      ch = getc(BookFile);
   } while ( ch != '\n' && !feof(BookFile) );
}
void DisplayAllBooks (void)
{
   int i;
   for (i = 1; i <= LastBook; i++)
   {
      printf ("%2i ", i);
      DisplayOneBook (book[i]);
   }
}
void DisplayOneBook (books b)
{
   printf ("%s %4i %7.2f\n", b.title, b.year, b.price );
}
void SwapBooks (int FirstIndex, int SecondIndex)
{
   books temp;
   temp = book[FirstIndex];
   book[FirstIndex] = book[SecondIndex];
   book[SecondIndex] = temp;
}
```

Program 10.7 implements the complete sort algorithm – swapping elements is carried out by the function SwapPair and the additional code is simply to allow input from a file and output to the screen. If the input file from the previous example is provided to the program, the following output will result:

```
After sort:
 1 Reflections on the Revolution in France     1790  157.00
 2 The Ginger Man                              1956    3.95
 3 The Education of a Poker Player             1957    5.95
 4 The Physics of Vibrations and Waves         1961    9.99
 5 Zen and the Art of Motorcycle Maintenance   1974    4.99
 6 The 35mm Photographer's Handbook            1979   15.95
 7 Pascal for Science and Engineering          1983   19.99
 8 Chambers 20th Century Thesaurus             1983   21.99
```

As before, the program will handle up to 20 entries in the input file – any further entries will be ignored.

SUMMARY OF CHAPTER 10

Key points

■ Structures allow us to group values of different types together in a single entity.

■ Assignment between structures is allowed only when they are of exactly the same type.

■ Testing equality between structures is never allowed, even when they have exactly the same type.

■ Structures passed as reference parameters to functions require the addressing operator (like simple variables, but unlike arrays). Similarly, the corresponding function header should indicate that the function expects an address rather than a value.

Good programming practice

■ If a set of values belong logically together, it is good practice to **encapsulate** them into a single data type, usually a structure. This means that, for example, only a single parameter representing the group of values has to be passed to functions.

■ Define a procedure for printing each structure involved in the program. This will be useful for debugging purposes as well as for producing normal output.

Common problems	
Problem	**Symptom**
Mismatch when scanning data in text file into a structure. For example, it is easy to miscount the characters in a string, when reading a line of data that contains a mixture of types.	Too many or too few characters can be read into strings, digits can be lost on numeric values, etc.

Problem *(continued)*	Symptom *(continued)*
Moving a single member of a structure to a new position in a table instead of moving the whole structure.	The association between the members of the structure is lost and nonsensical results will be produced.
Failure to use a reference parameter when a function is to change the members of a structure.	The function in question will change a local copy of the structure concerned and the changes will not be transmitted back to the calling code.

Debugging **tip**

■ Print all the members of suspect structures at critical stages of the program: after input from files, after complex manipulations, on entry to and exit from functions, and so on.

EXERCISES FOR CHAPTER 10

(1) Write a program which reads 10 pairs of numbers from a file, each pair representing the waist size (integer) and leg length (float) of jeans. The user of the program should be able to type in a waist size and find out whether there are any jeans in stock with that size waist, and if so, what leg sizes are available for that waist.

(2) In maths, a complex number has two parts, called the real part and the imaginary part. Write a function to add two complex numbers, where adding is carried out by simply adding the real part of one number to the real part of the other number to give the real part of the result. Similarly, the imaginary part of the result is obtained by adding the imaginary parts of the two inputs. Use a structure with two members, both of which are of type `float`, to represent a complex number.

(3) Write a function:

```
dates DaysBetween(dates date1, dates date2);
```

that finds the number of days between two dates.

(4) Using the structure definition

```
typedef struct {float x; float y} point;
```

show how a function can accept two points and return the distance between the two points.

(5) Another way of ensuring that the item in an array with the next-largest key is taken to the end of the unsorted section of the array is to scan through the unsorted section comparing each consecutive pair of elements in turn, swapping any pairs that are in the wrong order. Replacing the central part of the sort algorithm in Program 10.7 with a piece of program based on this approach gives rise to the so-called 'bubble sort'. Modify Program 10.7 so that it implements a bubble sort.

(6) Find out what a 'binary chop' method for searching is, and implement such a search.

(7) A day's weather record can be represented by a structure with seven members: three integers representing the date (day, month, year), the name of the meteorologist on duty that day (a string of up to 12 characters), followed by three floats representing hours of sunshine, rainfall in millimetres and midday temperature in degrees.

A file contains a text version of the weather data for the last year. Write a program that reads this data into a table and then repeatedly answers queries about the data from the user. Examples of the queries that might be available (from a menu) are:

- List the dates when a given meteorologist was on duty.
- Find all the wet days (your definition of wet).
- Find all the sunny days (your definition of sunny).
- Plot a graph showing the year's temperatures (see Chapter 9, Exercise 5).
- Plot a graph showing the year's rainfall.
- Plot a graph showing the year's sunshine.

(8) Write a program that implements a simple English–French dictionary (or a dictionary for any other pair of languages with which you are familiar). Each entry in the dictionary should be a structure with members representing an English word, a French word and an indication of the 'part of speech' of the word (noun, verb, etc.). The program should read the dictionary from a text file and then respond to a sequence of requests from a user to look up a word and provide the corresponding word (or words) in the other language, together with an indication of whether the words found are nouns, verbs, and so on.

C keywords

None of the following keywords can be used by the C programmer as a name for a variable or a function. The keywords used in this book appear in bold type.

auto	**double**	int	**struct**
break	**else**	**long**	**switch**
case	enum	register	**typedef**
char	extern	**return**	union
const	**float**	short	unsigned
continue	**for**	signed	**void**
default	goto	sizeof	volatile
do	**if**	static	**while**

There are a further 38 keywords in C++ which may not be allowed as variable names, depending on your particular system.

Arithmetic, relational and logical operators

Operator	Order of precedence	Definition
!	1	Logical 'not'
&	1	Take the address of ...
*	1	Take the contents of ...
*	2	Multiplication
/	2	Division
%	2	Remainder after integer division
+	3	Addition
–	3	Subtraction
<	4	Less than
>	4	Greater than
<=	4	Less than or equal to
>=	4	Greater than or equal to
==	5	Equal to
!=	5	Not equal to
&&	6	Logical 'and'
||	7	Logical 'or'

For clarity we have omitted three other 'operations' which are covered in this book. These are:

- `f( )`: applying a function
- `a[ ]`: selecting an element of an array
- `s.m`: selecting a member of a structure

These are all of equal priority, and have a higher priority than any of the other operators.

As mentioned in Section 2.3, the assignment operator and the abbreviated assignment operators can be used freely in expressions, but we discourage this practice.

Some library functions

■ Input–output functions

#include <stdio.h>

```
scanf("format codes", &variable1, &variable2, ...);
```

Format code	Type of value read
%i	int
%d	int
%f	float
%c	char
%s	string

```
printf("format codes and text", expression1, expression2, ...);
```

Format code example	Type of value output
%i	int
%4i	int, four characters
%05i	int, five characters, leading zeros instead of spaces
%d	Equivalent to %i
%f	float
%.2f	float, two digits after decimal point
%7.2f	float, seven characters, two after decimal point
%c	char
%s	string

```
FILE *filename;
```
    Declare a file variable, `filename`.

```
filename = fopen("TESTDATA.DAT","r");
```
    Open a file:
    `"TESTDATA.DAT"` is the DOS file name.
    `"r"` means for reading (`"w"` means writing).
    `filename` is the C file variable name.

```
fscanf(filename, "format codes", &variable1, &variable2, ...);
```
    As for `scanf`, but read from a file.
    `filename` must have been opened previously.

```
fprintf(filename, "format codes", expression1, expression2, ...);
```
    As for `printf`, but write to a file.
    `filename` must have been opened previously.

```
fclose(filename);
```
    Close a file when no longer needed.

```
c = getchar();
```
    Read character from keyboard.
```
putchar(c);
```
    Output character to screen.
```
c = getc(filename);
```
    Read character from file.
```
putc(filename, c);
```
    Output character to file.
```
foef(filename);
```
    Returns TRUE if the end of the file has been read.
```
ungetc(c, stdin);
```
    Gives the character c back to the standard input source.
```
gets(s);
```
    Reads a string up to the end of the current line in the data.

■ Mathematical functions

#include <math.h>

- `fabs`: absolute value (that is, discard minus sign if any)
- `sin`: natural sine, argument must be in radians
- `cos`: natural cosine, argument in radians
- `exp`: `exp(x)` returns e raised to the xth power

- `log`: natural logarithm
- `sqrt`: square root
- `atan`: arctangent
- `pow`: `pow(a, b)` returns `a` raised to the power `b`
- `floor`: `floor(x)` returns integer below `x`
- `ceil`: `ceil(x)` returns integer above `x`

■ Character processing functions

`#include <ctype.h>`

- `isdigit(c)`: returns TRUE if `c` is a numeric digit 0–9
- `isalpha(c)`: returns TRUE if `c` is an alphabetic character
- `isalnum(c)`: returns TRUE if `c` is either of the above
- `isupper(c)`: returns TRUE if `c` is an upper-case letter
- `islower(c)`: returns TRUE if `c` is a lower-case letter
- `ispunct(c)`: returns TRUE if `c` is a punctuation character

■ String processing functions

`#include <string.h>`

- `strlen (str)`: returns the length of the string
- `strcpy (str, "Some text")`: copies `"Some text"` into `str`
- `strcmp(str1, str2)`: returns TRUE if `str1` is the same as `str2`

■ Other standard library functions

`#include <stdlib.h>`

`#include <time.h>`

- `randomize();`: initializes the random number generator
- `random(n)`: an expression that evaluates to a random integer in the range 0 to n-1

Index